THE CRYSTAL GUIDEBOOK FOR LIGHTWORKERS

by Rebecca Steele

Published 2017

ISBN 978-0-646-96917-6

Typesetting services by Gunn & Penn Press

Global distribution services by Ingram Spark

facebook.com/RebeccaSteeleCrystals

None of the ideas, rituals or suggested practices contained in this book should be used as a substitute for professional medical treatment. Please consult a medical practitioner. This book is for entertainment purposes only. No responsibility can be accepted for any loss, injury or inconvenience sustained by any person, business, or organization using this book for any reason.

For all old souls
and their burdens

contents

introduction

Crystals have been used for centuries as decorations, adornments and in healing or worship rituals. No matter what your passion, if you are into crystals, then this book is for you!

Designed for the lightworker using principals that relate to today's life, this book provides practical information about everyday crystal use. Inside you will find details setting out the 68 essential crystals for primary use in lightwork. Alongside this, you will find 138 focus elements distributed across 13 realms of practice, as well as practical guidelines on crystal selection and care.

Using the guidelines and practice notes, you can learn how to:

- ⊢ change the flow of energy
- ⊢ improve your general state of wellbeing
- ⊢ identify choices and facilitate decision making
- ⊢ improve your self-knowledge
- ⊢ target areas that need development
- ⊢ achieve profound change

Included are instructions for some popular crystal uses such as beacons and jewelry, as well rituals such as grids that you can use to help focus on various aspects of your life. Whether you use this book for healing or personal development - knowledge and change are within your power.

Enjoy the process and have fun in the journey, as you discover the wonderful world of crystals.

the lightworker

There are dozens of descriptions of lightwork – all positive and beautiful – but what does being a lightworker really mean? And how does it relate to crystals?

In a textbook sense, a lightworker could be described as a philosopher. Or maybe a counselor, with a little bit of healer thrown in. A soothsayer perhaps. Whatever the explanation, lightworkers have a few things in common: we are aware of nature and that, like nature, all things have a lifecycle that constantly changes, continually evolves, and almost always could do with a little help.

That help doesn't always mean hands-on treatment of some ailment. While lightworkers always want to heal, sometimes there is nothing about us that is broken or needs fixing – it just needs some tweaking or some improvement. A little pearl of wisdom that puts us back on our life journey and helps us on our way.

In lightwork, the clue is in the name – lightworkers have discovered how to live in the "light". It's that state of being that is weightless, effortless, and luminous while still being curious and thirsty for knowledge. It's where all things have a meaning but not all things need to have sound reasoning. It just...well, is.

To work our craft, lightworkers have many tools available – cards, symbols, stones, numbers, planets, intuition – the list goes on. Some may seem logical and grounded, others just plain weird and nonsensical. There are also many tried and true activities such as Feng Shui and Smudging, and all kinds of therapy from Reiki to Tai Chi. Almost every culture has its own energy lightwork occupation. Some are ancient and some are more aligned to today's world.

The common belief in all of these is that there is a greater force present. A life force if you like. While that may be scientifically the hardest thing to prove, lightworkers are true believers in what lies beyond just science and theology. Call it our spirituality maybe, but we're all put on this earth to do good. We're here to acknowledge and work within the light, help others and protect that which is precious and sacred. Lightworkers take up the reins for something that is profound and beautiful.

amethyst clusters

living in the light

There is nothing more beautiful than holding in your hand a tiny piece of nature's wonder – a colorful little crystal that appears to have no godly reason for being. It's a complex system of just the right minerals and elements, together in one moment in time, under the most perfect and often most extreme conditions, and out pops this glorious testament to our earth's ability to create lasting beauty. A gift of light and energy fused together in a crystal.

In working in the light with crystals, the fundamental belief is that crystals resonate with earth's energy, which is true of every living thing. These precious little stones – not made of man – present the earth's life force captured in stone. They are in fact its purest form, being earthborn anomalies.

In practice, being present in the energy that crystals represent and radiate, is considered holistically beneficial. On its own, the symbolism of a sole crystal enables you to focus on aspects of your life that cannot otherwise be addressed by traditional means. That focus helps you to understand and connect with your authentic self. Who are you? Why are you here? How and what do you communicate? How do you relate to the world around you? These are all good questions.

Crystal work is a facilitator of change and profound change can only come about with focus. What crystal work allows is that needed focus in a very positive way. Seemingly, it works. It's beyond scientific basis or proof. The positive impact the world of crystals brings enables us to break through.

Crystal work is only as beneficial as your faith will allow. What's most important, and significant, is that you believe in something and that your beliefs provide a positive influence in your life in some way.

fact and fiction

Skepticism is always healthy in all aspects of your belief systems and questioning your beliefs can often be personal and/or external. The hardest thing for anyone to fathom in crystal practice is the constant struggle between sciences, theology, and spirituality.

Most critics of crystals cite the absence of scientific evidence or simply dismiss them as hocus-pocus, being a contrarian distraction from other, more substance based beliefs. Outside of science and religion sits the esoteric metaphysical world of the lightworker. That which cannot be explained by theory or proof, or words written in history.

There is no science behind crystal work, nor does there need to be. You believe the earth is round and that it revolves around the sun – science has proven that. But it was once believed the earth was flat. That did no-one any harm either. Science will continue to prove, disprove and re-prove its own basis, and that's its real purpose.

Religion has provided guidebooks for the millions. Again there is no science to prove that anything in religion is true. It's generally based on scripture and folklore that has been handed down through the ages. What is proven is that religion is destined, if not designed, to provide both a path and comfort in our daily lives. It is our soul protection.

It doesn't matter whether your beliefs are based in science or scripture - or an ever changing, often conflicting mix of the two. Science is not always right and is often disproven. Religious doctrine takes many forms, some of which are as valid, or obscure as your beliefs in the power of crystals. All are valid in such that all serve one purpose – to make your life, and the life of others, better. And all means all.

choosing crystals

There are hundreds of different crystals and they come in a kaleidoscope of colors and forms. Sometimes this can be overwhelming when trying to decide which ones to buy.

In this book, 68 crystals are identified as keystones for crystal work, although you can always add others depending on which you are drawn too.

The general rule of thumb is that crystals choose you. When shopping for crystals, be aware when drawn to a particular crystal and keep your mind open when browsing.

rose quartz roughs

size

A crystal's ability is not determined by size. Some of the smallest stones will demonstrate energy equal to larger stones. However, larger stones are preferable when used in a beacon, smaller tumbled stones when used in grid making or jewelry such that one stone does not drown out another.

imperfections

Some crystals have imperfections that convey special meanings such as phantoms where a crystal appears to be set inside another crystal which is highly prized in things such as quartz. Other imperfections such as depressions or keyholes also indicate higher meanings and add the crystal's elemental ability.

For this reason, it is best to view a crystal from all sides and to hold it in your hand, hold it up to the light and feel its weight.

rough or polished

Crystals can be rough, polished and clustered and come in a variety of shapes. Polished crystals provide the most convenience for everyday use and are the most common. Polished crystals are simply rough crystals that have been placed in a tumbler with a special medium such as crushed walnut shells, to remove the rough edges and provide the smooth polished surface.

Roughs are in their most natural form and can be useful when looking for increased energy. They often lack the beauty of polished crystals but are of the same metaphysical value.

imitations

Some stones sold as crystals are nothing more than manufactured colored glass or heat treated crystals of lesser value. For example, stones such as obsidian can often be purchased in a variety of unnatural colors including pink and blue. These are most likely simply manufactured colored glass. However, substitution is fine especially where specific crystals are hard to come by.

Other crystals are branded and sold under a trade name. Bolivianite, which is actually a mix of amethyst and citrine, is an example and may communicate elements that are different to those expected.

It's recommended that you try to determine the authenticity of crystals to ensure you are buying good stones. A reputable seller should always state whether the stone is natural, treated or manufactured. If you're in doubt, always ask. Good sellers will be aware of the origins of their stones and very likely happy to tell you all about them.

caring for crystals

Crystals are made up of naturally occurring minerals that have been fused together under enormous pressure and extreme heat, deep within the earth. It is worth remembering that most crystals found today were formed thousands, if not millions of years ago and carry with them all of the history of the earth from which they were created.

No two crystals will be alike and the degradation or destruction of a crystal is final and will require it to be replaced. With this in mind, crystals should be treated as living objects and shown appropriate care.

scratching

Most crystals are fairly resilient to knocks and bumps, however, you should take care to avoid mixing rough stones with polished stones as this may cause chipping or scratches on the surface. To prevent damage, wrap your crystals individually or store them in containers such as ice cube trays or egg cartons.

If a crystal is too chipped, scratched or becomes dull with use, replace it.

chrysoprase tumble stones

immersion

Some crystals will tolerate being immersed in liquids however others will not. Some are sensitive to water and may become cloudy, lose or change color or in some cases dissolve completely. Others can contain minerals that may be harmful with prolonged exposure or if consumed. For these reasons, immersing crystals for any purpose is not recommended.

As a rule, you should never need to immerse a crystal in any liquid unless it has become encrusted with dirt, in which case it should be replaced.

cleaning

With handling, crystals will pick up oils, which in turn will attract dirt and dust. To clean your crystals, wipe them over with a soft natural cloth, preferably cotton or flannel, dampened with ordinary tap water. Use warm water if required to remove oils. Never use commercial cleaning chemicals of any kind.

smudging

Where crystals have been exposed to negative energy or where a crystal's performance seems to have weakened, prepare a smudge bath by placing them on a cloth and passing a lit smudge stick over and around them. Use a feather to blow the smoke over them. This will draw out any negativity energy and carry it away in the smoke.

Smudge sticks are generally made of white sage and come in many sizes. They are readily available from most metaphysical shops or online. Ensure the herbs used have been gathered from a sustainable source and, where possible, prepared using Native American traditions. Be careful not to burn your crystals by placing them too close to the smudge or to candles as they may break.

keep it natural

The trick with crystal care is to keep it as simple and as natural as possible. This way your crystals should remain as new for many years. Look after them as they look after you.

activating crystals

Preparing your stones for realm and elemental work is a fairly simple process. You can use them as they are, however you will get heightened power and energy from crystals that have been activated.

Setting your stones in sunlight for a time is a common method. A nice spot on a kitchen shelf will do. However, some crystals are sensitive to sunlight and you may see some colors fade if left sitting too long or exposed repeatedly.

The best method for programming or activating your crystals is to leave them exposed in the light of a full moon for a few hours. Make sure they are out of the weather and always try for times when the moon has fully risen and at its sharpest. While night time is usually best, sometimes the moon will be visible at its fullest during daylight hours. Choose what is most convenient for you.

Those who practice astrology may also energize certain crystals with reference to the planets viewable in the sky at the time.

Before and after activation, give your crystals a gentle wipe over to remove any traces of dirt and oils. Avoid using chemically impregnated cloths such as lens cleaners. Opt instead for a soft cotton or flannel cloth made damp with ordinary tap water.

From time to time, give your crystals a boost by repeating the activation process.

using your crystals

You can use crystals in a variety of ways, from divination to healing and so on. This book focuses on crystal use that is particular to lightwork such as beacons, poles, jewelry, and grids.

beacons

Crystal beacons offer a guiding light and their use in the home or workplace can form an intrinsic connection to the spiritual realms.

A beacon is a major crystal or a group of crystals that is placed prominently on display in your home or workplace. Not only decorative and beautiful to look at, a beacon can also provide a continual source of positive energy and radiation while absorbing or repelling negative energies.

Single clusters or geodes are common beacons and they can be simple and small, or grand and elaborate. If you don't have a major crystal, you can build a beacon using a number of selected crystals arranged together in a basket or on a shelf.

For display, choose crystals that resonate with you, or pair and swap them as you want, to intensify certain elements. If your beacon has one or more sides facing a wall, place a small mirror behind it to reflect its energy for the fullest effect.

When you need to temporarily amplify the energy, place a small candle near the beacon or place it under a lampshade.

poles

Crystal poles are easy to construct and need only be tiny in order to radiate energy. Gather the crystals you desire and place them in the corners of a room, preferably away from windows.

A good home pole would be to place small rose quartz crystals in the corners of the house to attract and radiate love, or howlite crystals for harmony. Always make sure they are out of the reach of children and pets.

Clean and reactivate pole crystals occasionally.

keepsakes

To keep crystals close by, but not on display, find small ones or flats that will fit into your pocket, purse or wallet. This way you can mix and swap, and use them whenever you're out and about.

jewelry

Most crystals can be made into wearable jewelry. You can either buy them already fashioned into set pieces or make them yourself using simple jewelry findings and some good jewelry glue or crystal clay.

Consider renovating an old piece of jewelry or buy the base settings from a good jewelry supplier. Pendants, lanyards, bracelets, rings, brooches and earrings are all good as well as hair combs and even nail art for tiny crystals. Use silver cage pendants to swap crystals for daily use.

grids

Crystal grids are perhaps the most exciting form of lightwork with crystals, beyond healing therapies. Grids come in all sizes and forms and can be personal or constructed with a group of friends.

A basic grid layout has four corners and a central soul stone with focus stones placed in areas around it, according to what type of grid you are setting.

In the later pages, you'll find some layout examples for setting crystal grids.

combining & pairing

The 68 essential crystals are arranged in the following categories. Look for these symbols in the crystal listings for quick reference.

clearing
To remove obstacles and provide clear pathways

energizing
To provide energy to the desired outcomes

grounding
To gather knowledge or foster understanding

protecting
To safeguard the element or outcome

Each crystal is categorized according to its major influence. When deciding which crystals will deliver the greatest focus, you can pair crystals and elements that correspond to the focus or outcome you want.

examples

If working on the "devotion" element in the virtuous realm you can use its foundation crystal, pink calcite which is a clearing crystal. This will help you to remove obstacles and affirm your commitment to a goal. To this you could also add an energizing crystal such as peridot to provide happy energy to the affirmation. If the goal is to be prosperous and enduring, then include chrysoprase. Alternatively, if the goal is to understand where your devotion lies, then pair with labradorite.

In some cases, such as in a simple ley grid, you may want to use many of the same crystals. For example, when working on elements that relate to love alone, use a variety of rose quartz crystals.

Crystal combinations are neither pre-set nor limited, and you can use a single crystal or many. Finding combinations is the fun part of crystal work and along the way, you will discover what works for you and gives you the most positive benefit.

carnelian tumble stones

symbols

You can use your crystals just about anywhere you like, however, constraints such as brittleness may prevent recommended use in some areas. As a guide only, look for these symbols in the crystal listings for quick reference.

grids

Arrange or include in crystal grids. See the section on grid building for best use.

poles

Single crystals of any size, placed in the corners of rooms or in any area that is contained by walls.

beacons

Arrange crystals in a group and place together in your home or workplace.

jewelry and keepsakes

Set crystals in pendants, brooches, bracelets, earrings, hair combs, and rings. For keepsakes, place small crystals in your pocket, purse or wallet and carry them with you.

immersion

Safe to be immersed in water.

sunlight

Safe to be exposed to prolonged sunlight.

heat

Safe to be exposed to prolonged heat.

durability

Reasonably resilient to damage.

the elements

Set out on the following pages are 138 elements, grouped into 13 crystal realms. These will guide you through using crystals in your lightwork. The 68 essential crystals are detailed in a later section.

Each element contains a basic statement about its core influence. This is followed by a crystal (or crystals) recommended for use when focusing on the chosen element.

The recommended crystal is only a suggestion and you may find other crystals that are appropriate also. That's entirely up to you and, with practice, you'll become more aware of what works, and what doesn't. At the very least, choose a crystal that relates to one of the four purposes: clearing, energizing, grounding, or protecting depending on what elemental outcome you are trying to achieve.

Next, there is a suggested use. Again, depending on the type of stone you are using, you may find other ways to use your crystals. Be mindful here of the care limitations such as immersion, exposure to sunlight etc. You can interchange crystals as needed, again depending on your desired use.

Lastly, each element has some practice notes. These are here to guide you through the element – what it stands for, what to focus on and how to focus. Sometimes you will discover additional elements need to be worked in conjunction, or maybe as a prerequisite.

As you work with the elements, have some fun experimenting with different layouts and combinations. Take your time and don't rush it. These stones may have been around for millions of years, they may not give up their qualities or wisdom in a hurry. Share your findings with friends and above all, enjoy living in the light!

affirmation realm

abundance

Attract abundance, where one particular thing or everything, is plentiful and many choices are apparent.

crystal epidote, magnesite

practice There are things you want in your life - and things you'd rather not have. This is easily recognized, yet it's possible to be constrained by the distinction between the very two. While you may assume abundance means you are surrounded by good things, it can also mean you are inundated with bad things. As such, when focusing on abundance you need to be clear about what it is you want, and not focus on what you don't want. "I want to be wealthy" rather than "I don't want to be poor" would be a good example of the distinction.

The ability to attract the very things you desire and dispel those you don't can be helped by first understanding what is in your life at the present. How did you get the things you love? How do you get more of those? Do you have everything you want and do you want everything you have? Abundance comes in many forms – material things, relationships or influences, and it can appear as any one of those.

In moving toward an abundant life you need to discard or lessen the negatives and focus on activities that build on the things you see as having a positive influence.

affirmation

Affirm or encourage a particular life situation or event. Use an affirmation crystal to strengthen beliefs and commitment to goals.

crystal clear quartz

practice In a busy world, it is easy to get distracted from the intended path or to forget core beliefs. This is especially true when your beliefs are not strong and are easily influenced by others. Affirmations serve as subtle, yet powerful reminders of your aims and beliefs. They allow you to focus and live in the here and now.

Affirmations should not lead you to be single-minded which will eventually block you to other opportunities. Instead, affirmations should simply reiterate your life intentions and bring them into the foreground of your thought processes. They can be used to alter habitual negative behaviors and to encourage alternative positive behaviors that will ultimately lead to change.

creativity

Form something new, including new ideas and find ways to move forward.

crystal pyrite

practice When in a rut or a situation that is stale, a new perspective is needed. To unblock the barriers that will enable you to move forward, you must be creative in your thinking. Creativity allows you to explore new things, change thinking and see things in a new light. It enables you to move in a new direction.

Being creative in your thoughts does not always mean discarding the old in favor of something new. Creativity can simply allow you to see the old in a new way. However, in some cases, this may lead to the abandonment of old thinking, which is an acceptable outcome.

Allowing your mind to be creative stimulates new life in the way a tree drops leaves in the autumn to allow new growth in the spring. Where shall I grow a new branch? What will it look like?

Creativity flows when energy is stimulated, allowing enthusiasm and curiosity to govern your thought processes.

empowerment

Gain confidence in your ability to undertake tasks, or take an initiative in a difficult situation.

crystal hypersthene, smoky quartz

practice Empowerment is different to strength. When you have the ability to undertake tasks but feel powerless to do so, you can work on empowerment to unlock the barrier that prevents you from moving forward. A lack of empowerment can be due to low confidence, overwhelming fear or apathy, or plain circumstance. Sometimes all that is needed is a fresh approach.

Empowerment comes when you understand what is holding you back and why. These barriers may not be insurmountable, and in many cases may be trivial. As opportunities arise, overcoming negative influence is a process of transforming ability into action, bypassing or dismissing the behaviors that lead you to do nothing. It is only then you can move forward instinctively.

inner peace

Calm your mind and find freedom from negative emotions such as anger, resentment, hatred, and fear. Find forgiveness, be comfortable and at ease with your innermost thoughts.

crystal apatite, green fluorite

practice In a perfect spiritual state, you would view all things equally, with the same amount of emotion and opinion. However, your very human nature means that you will often collect disparate thoughts, seeing everything as standalone objects, each worthy of its own view. This can create inner chaos as you try to juggle the vast range of your capabilities and the many objects you are able to gather. Soon you can be overwhelmed and there is conflict.

In finding inner peace you must gather the objects of your negative emotions and put them in a single place. Then you can see beyond them to reveal your authentic self and this is where you can find inner peace.

requests

Seek fulfillment of hopes through prayer to a higher being or authority. Make requests to beings in the higher realm such as spirit guides.

crystal vulcanite

practice Making requests or affirming your beliefs often requires that you seek assistance from a higher power. Sometimes your personal affirmations are not sufficient or you simply need to acknowledge influences in the higher realm. This may be God, a saint or a guide, or any entity that you deem to be an enlightened higher authority.

You should try to identify the higher power and affirm directly, otherwise, a request affirmation can be put to the universe if no single higher authority can be found, or is considered appropriate. Hold during meditation or prayer or when asking for specific things during grid work. Wear as jewelry to maintain a connection to higher beings.

serenity

Develop a state where all is as it should be, even when it may not be all that you want or need. See things as they truly are and learn to accept.

crystal shungite

practice Serenity can be seen as living in the moment where everything is at peace and all things are as they should be.

While you can work on things that require change, and you can also work to accept the here and now, not everything can be changed in an instant.

In developing a serene state, be conscious of both the current situation – "it is" – and how you want it to be – "it can be". Affirming serenity, or accepting the current situation is a pre-requisite to any desired change.

awareness realm

awareness

Gain appreciation or further understanding of an external situation. Garner knowledge and open your mind to external messages.

crystal sardonyx, vulcanite

practice Opening your consciousness to external inputs enables you to add to your knowledge. A closed mind, or beliefs that are too closely held can lead you to be dogmatic and inflexible, possibly limiting your spiritual growth. In increasing awareness, you are really opening yourself to new ideas, thereby increasing your ability to change and move forward. It helps you to understand the current situation and past influences on an everyday level.

In mediumship, receiving messages is wholly dependent on developing awareness, allowing channels to open and flow. Blockages can be due to forced, misunderstood beliefs that may hinder that flow. In such cases, the medium is encouraged to work on opening awareness.

consciousness

Gain appreciation, knowledge or further understanding of a situation that is internal. Gather knowledge and open your mind to internal messages, including emotions and health.

crystal kunzite, sardonyx

practice Your internal thoughts are central to your being. Without referring to your own internal beliefs you can behave in ways that seem contrary to what you actually believe.

In the physical world, your body tells you when to eat, rest, sleep and be active. These triggers are innate, developing from birth. As you get older and fill your life with activities, you become less aware of your own thoughts and more reactive to events, without ever understanding why. This can happen on a physical or emotional level.

In focusing on consciousness, you begin to understand and develop trust in your own ideas and beliefs. It also strengthens and refines any personal goals you may have.

higher self

Develop awareness of your higher self, beyond daily activities and environmental influences. Understand who you are and where your true beliefs lie as influenced by a higher power.

crystal sardonyx

practice Much of your belief system will come from life experience as you fashion your ideas learned in events from birth through to adulthood. However, there is often a higher power in play – you do things you know to be true even though you have no experience or knowledge of them. This may manifest as things such as caring, fear, paternal instincts or such. In this case, you are influenced by your higher self which provides your most basic human instincts. Traits emanating from the higher self are difficult to change – they are not inherited or learned. They are naturally instinctive, presenting differently in each person. Sometimes they are strong and sometimes weak or absent.

An ability to distinguish between awareness based on your DNA, and awareness based on your experience allows you to connect these most instinctive common thoughts and become aware of how they impact you.

illumination

Reveal and understand your personal gifts and talents that may be unique or strong.

crystal kunzite, peridot

practice What makes some people better with numbers and others better with creativity? Why do some people appear wise despite being seemingly uneducated? We all have personal talents that make us different from one another.

When combined with your beliefs, those talents make you unique. You may be drawn along a certain path that does not suit your talents and yet you still feel a sense of yearning for something different. "I enjoy my office job and I've learned to be good at it, yet I still feel most comfortable when I'm out in nature. I feel at odds."

In focusing on illuminating your hidden gifts, you are really trying to remove barriers, allowing yourself to be curious and explore. They may not appear immediately and you may try many things and discard others. The universe may need you to gather knowledge before revealing what may be hidden, in such a way that you can understand.

intuition

Develop an ability to understand things instinctively without the need for reasoning. Help to distinguish between what is authentic and what is deceptive.

crystal nuummite

practice When something feels right or true, yet you have no hard evidence to support it, you are using your intuitive instinct to govern your thoughts. That instinct can be learned or innate.

It may be that you never need to provide reasoning, however, in order to grow your intuition, you should also be open to questioning what your instinctive messages mean and how you should interpret them.

Developing intuition in part means learning to trust yourself and your thoughts, so working on other aspects of awareness would also be beneficial.

Intuition is a key component in mediumship.

past lives

Seek information on prior self-incarnations and understand how they shape your current behavior.

crystal lapis lazuli, pietersite

practice The information you have to conduct your daily life comes from many sources. It can be intuitive or learned. When a thought process or behavior cannot be explained by either, it is possible the information has been passed on from a previous life, of which you are unaware.

Working on past lives can expose those sources and enable you to determine how they govern your current day. Is there more to be learned? Have you used the information in an appropriate way?

In some instances, past life influences can have a negative effect on your life. In these cases, the past life may have had issues that were unresolved in his/her lifetime and may have been passed to you to resolve.

Positive influences can be interpreted as positive experiences that were so profound in the past life as to warrant them being passed on to future beneficiaries.

potential

Seek to reveal and fulfill your potential, or to achieve the best outcome in a personal situation.

crystal epidote, pyrite

practice Many of your actions will be actions of habit without needing any conscious thought of why or how. In this case, you are not focused on potential.

Consider it this way – life is a wall of pigeon holes. In each hole, there is a message – a life experience or piece of knowledge. As you investigate the pigeon holes at random, you gather information that you can use going forward. When you are aware of potential, each message can have some potential use. It may not be understood or used it immediately, but it may be useful in the future. Each has potential that you can build on.

Building self-awareness is key to revealing your potential. If you don't know what you are capable of, then you will never do it – you will never enter that pigeon-hole or you will miss the message it holds.

With information, you have the best opportunity to move forward in a direction that enables you to receive good outcomes.

reflection

Understand the consequences of actions, both yours and others, and how reactions affect you. Look back to the past to find answers to current issues.

crystal lapis lazuli, sardonyx

practice In relationships people are often like mirrors, reflecting back the behaviors and thoughts of others. At times, this creates both harmony and conflict. Am I happy because I'm surrounded by happy people? Or is my happiness my own doing? The same can be asked of sadness or discontent.

The reflection element aids understanding of external influences, and whether those influences are inspiring or clouding your own path. Reflection also helps you to look back to events in the past to help understand how they have shaped the present day.

Ideally, when you look in a mirror, the reflection you see should only be yourself. Here you find true authenticity. Authenticity does not mean instantly discarding external influences – just understanding how they make you who you are.

selflessness

Dismiss selfish behaviors and attune to others needs and situations.

crystal sunstone

practice This is the opposite of reflection. If you are too closed to external influences, you may appear selfish as you have nothing to project other than your own thoughts, behaviors, and opinions. To move forward you must be able to receive some influence from those around you, both negative and positive.

Being aware of selflessness helps you to build empathy and understanding of other people and how they interact with you. If you receive criticism and you feel bad, is the person giving the criticism to blame? Or is your unease your own doing? This does not mean you need to heed the others person's words, but simply control how they affect you.

Discovering selflessness helps to put your own thoughts and opinions aside, allowing you to truly connect with the situations of others. When trying to attract positive outcomes you must first open yourself to external influence.

Mediums and lightworkers will both benefit from this element.

soul awakening

Become aware of a higher purpose, a greater universe or raising a belief that you exist beyond the physical world.

crystal peridot, yellow opal

practice Your soul is the very essence of your existence on a spiritual level. It is born with you or may have morphed from a past life. Throughout life, your soul receives messages that shape and alter your behavior. As you make your way in the world, it becomes your own internal book of collected knowledge.

The soul does not reside in the physical world – it has a higher purpose. It cannot be contrived or altered with mental therapy. The soul only accepts and stores information that is pure and required, filtering out what is common sense or everyday experience. And you cannot, in life, be separated from your soul.

In working on soul awakening you are trying to tap into the wisdom your soul holds, being aware of its existence and purity.

spiritual awareness

Understand true inner beliefs and become attuned to the natural world.

crystal sardonyx, vulcanite

practice Almost all of your crystal work is helping to promote your spiritual awareness, to bring it to the foreground and help your understanding.

As you become more aware, you begin to strengthen your beliefs and it allows you to move forward in a more harmonious way. You accept your roles in nature and attune to the natural movement of the earth. You are influenced by things such as the moon, the seasons, and the environment. You can more readily connect with the animal kingdom. You accept that you are just part of the cycle of life.

Profound change begins with raising your spiritual awareness as you accept that your spirit is open and available to change. New ideas are formed, your beliefs grow and become clear.

spiritual development

Seek to increase your spirituality, to raise or become open to new beliefs or fresh ideas. Develop an affinity with the natural world.

crystal black onyx

practice From birth, you are naturally open to learning. This is the gift of life. However, as you age that openness gradually decreases. Your body of knowledge becomes a cluttered mountain of experiences, some of which you will believe are the only possible outcomes to similar situations, and you become prejudiced. Eventually, you risk becoming completely closed, fixed in your beliefs and lifestyle, and unable to develop any further.

To unlock your spirituality and continue learning, you must be able to discard old experiences where necessary, having learned what you can from them. With this, you can change and grow. Everything, no matter how grand, weird, or out of character – becomes possible.

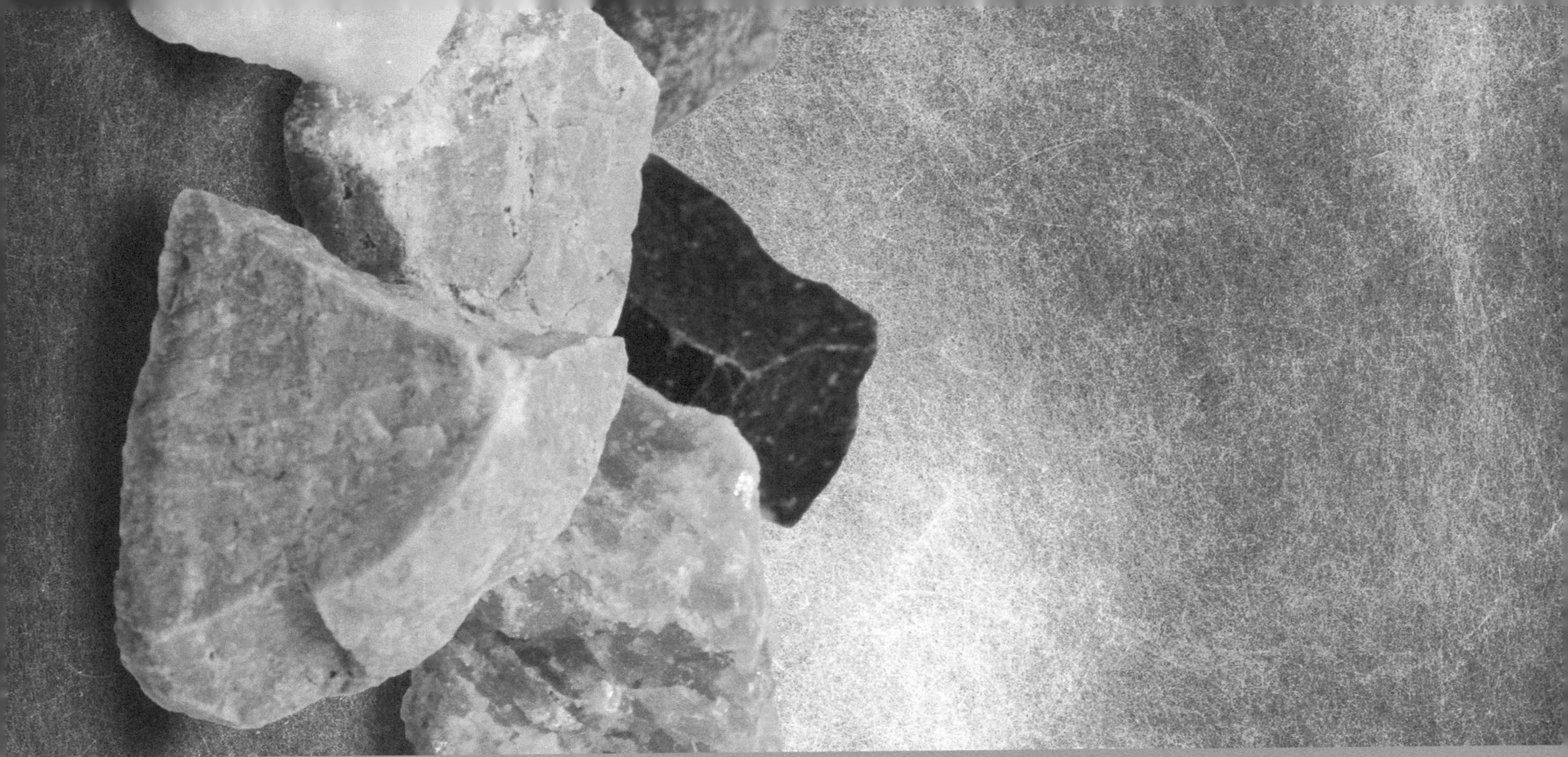

emotional realm

belonging

Strengthen your sense of affinity with a subject or group and feel accepted. Connect with ancestors and strong family influences from the past.

crystal lapis lazuli

practice Participation in anything can sometimes lead to a feeling of disassociation or loneliness, especially if you don't feel accepted. In group activities, this sense can separate you from "the now" and you tend to dwell on negatives instead. Building self-confidence is key to such situations.

Finding belonging is not all about being around people that have common interests. Belonging is also about being comfortable in such groups, or even in being on your own.

In building a sense of belonging you can draw on your ancestors as this is one thing you have in common with everyone. We all come from somewhere that influences us. We all have a distinct "tribe" to which we unquestionably belong.

In order to strengthen today's sense of belonging, examining the past by undertaking some investigation of ancestry will be beneficial.

calm

Seek a feeling of serenity or low motion when external influences are chaotic.

crystal amazonite, shungite

practice You must balance a busy life with periods of calm such that your spirit can have time to rest and restore energy. If you don't experience periods of inactivity, you may burn out and/or be susceptible to negative influences coming from the world around you.

Calm can be obtained by stepping back, without contemplation of what is causing your unease. Simple meditation will assist. Once the spirit is relaxed and free of thoughts, you can gradually allow the noise to return in a more methodical way.

Wear as jewelry or carry a keepsake (shungite). Include in a grid when working on a specific problem. Useful if placed in the corners of a room or home where constant motion is disturbing.

comfort

Dismiss or alleviate feelings of distress or grief. Ease symptoms of pain or unease. Find support through periods of grief and loss.

crystal blue quartz, kyanite

practice Pain, whether emotional or physical, is a part of life. You can't journey through without experiencing some sort of pain at various times. In the emotional realm, pain caused by grief or loss can be consuming – being at the forefront of your thoughts all the time, without relenting. It often causes you to react in ways that appear abnormal.

Finding comfort means allowing yourself to experience pain as a natural emotion. It's okay to feel bad, to be sad about whatever has caused your grief. That's normal. Accept it, allow it to run its course. If you deny pain or allow it to take all of your attention, without recognizing that your unease is simply the necessary path your spirit must take, comfort will be missed or harder to obtain.

Pain is always temporary as you eventually revert to your natural human instincts, and you find comfort. In this you should not try to block it, rather allow it time.

divine love

Attune with a higher being, seek acceptance and forgiveness and acknowledge imperfections.

crystal rose quartz

practice Moving forward along your spiritual path will often see you in occasional whirlpools of self-doubt and conflict. If you become too sensitive to external influences that transmit negativity, you can become isolated and consumed, questioning everything you believe in. This is the time to seek and affirm love from higher powers.

In the higher realms, you are always accepted and loved for exactly who you are and everything you do. Acceptance and forgiveness are always available when you acknowledge divine love.

emotional blockages

Remove, resolve or hinder negative emotions from your thoughts, or in reactions to personal situations. Help to ease disruption, especially in relationships.

crystal jadeite, sodalite

practice As time goes by, your opinions and feelings on certain aspects of your life will change. This is especially true as you gather life experience. Sometimes these will be positive, other times less so. As you grow and change, so will your responses - even if the influences remain the same. You simply see things differently.

If you are feeling constrained or disrupted by thoughts of negativity, your relationship with the object or subject will cease to grow. Just dismissing the emotions and trying to press on will not solve the problem. Before you clear an emotional blockage, you must analyze the negative emotion and determine why it makes you feel the way it does. What has changed?

Confronting your disruptive responses may be unpleasant, however, there are things to be learned from all situations.

emotional stability

Enhance your ability to stay calm during times of pressure or stress. Learn to put yourself first.

crystal sodalite

practice Why do I crack under pressure? This is a question that rarely gets asked when you "lose it". Something happens and your emotions bubble up, manifesting as anger or sadness or any range of emotions in between. It's almost inexplicable at times. Yet you still never ask yourself – why do I react this way?

Find a quiet place to consider the thing or event that has made you uneasy. The natural position is to try to change the thing or dwell on the event. This is not a solution. Emotional stability comes from looking inward and accepting that you own your reactions. You may have no control over the thing or the event itself and in reality, it is not what is disrupting you.

Real change comes when you understand how you express your emotions and that you are the only one in control of the situation. With practice and inward observation, you will find stability.

grief

Work through periods of grief and ease feelings of sadness or stress. Understand and reconcile a state of loss.

crystal kyanite

practice No matter how much you value things in your life, you can't hold onto them forever. At times you will lose things that are dear to you and you will experience profound grief.

Grief is a process that is well documented. It cannot be hurried. You should not be expected to "just get over it" or to "move on with your life". These are hollow words to anyone who has lost something cherished.

If you break a bone, catch a cold or cut yourself, you generally accept that it will take some time to heal. You know what to do - how to dress a wound or how to rest and recuperate. This is healing in the physical world. However, you may be less aware of the process when the hurt exists only in the emotional realm. While it is real and often the hurt is deeper, its lack of physical appearance leads to misunderstanding.

In dealing with grief you should understand that it needs progression, a path to follow. It is the only way you can heal.

happiness

Ease feelings of sadness, isolation, and melancholy. Alleviate mood swings or understand low moods and what causes them.

crystal kunzite, peridot

practice Depression is a sign your spirit is out of balance with the physical world. Your spirit should be viewed as always "attempting" to find a happy balanced state. When your spirit is blocked or weak, you can become open to negative emotions. You may be advised to consider a radical change to overcome depressive thoughts, however, this often leads to disappointment and eventually you resume your bad habits.

Overcoming darker periods takes discipline, and this can be achieved in small steps. Each day you must allow your spirit its attempt to find a path to joy – even for a moment. It may be something as simple as taking a walk or reading a book – it must be a moment where you put your own negative emotions aside and consciously allow your spirit to emerge. In order to strengthen your spirit, feed it occasionally and then more often. Accept that it will take time and many different moments, until the balance is restored.

self esteem

Raise belief in your personal abilities and be confident in your self-worth. Help to build self-confidence and a belief in yourself.

crystal blue quartz, bronzite, pyrite, rose quartz

practice To find and appreciate your inner voice and raise your own perception of yourself, you must, of course, first be conscious of one thing – you. If you do not value yourself, you will be unable to place value in anything else.

Self-examination is often a difficult process and if it is undertaken in a negative way, it may lead to further issues. We all have potential and possibilities, and when we don't recognize this fact, those potentials and possibilities are masked and manifest as low self-esteem.

Self-esteem comes from within and it will be susceptible to negative external influence if your own spirit is weak. Learn to disregard how others see you, as their opinion is something you cannot control. You do, however, have complete control over your opinion of yourself. In order to move forward, you can only work on your own opinions and put yourself first. Building self-esteem will then enhance the relationships you have with the outside world.

self-healing

Dismiss negativity and attract positive energy to assist or speed recovery.

crystal kyanite

practice The power of positive influence cannot be underestimated when seeking to self-heal. When illness – mental or physical – overpowers you, you must consciously dismiss negativity that will weigh down the healing process.

If the hurt is extreme, then you must take direct action. Surround yourself with positive people. If there are people around you that provide you with negative input, step away for a while, or politely ask them to leave you be, until you have recovered.

This is also a time to make affirmations, resolve to break bad habits and to set goals.

worry

Seek to alleviate internal pressures and understand the triggers that cause them. Dismiss worry and accept things that are beyond your control or influence.

crystal jadeite, serpentine

practice Anxiety and worry are invasive emotions. They block the spirit's path to find natural happiness. Left unchecked, constant worrying can lead to bigger problems and may eventually manifest into a chronic disorder such as depression or panic attacks.

When worry takes over, there are messages that you need to understand or have yet to receive. Use crystals to understand what is worrying you and try to turn negative perceptions into positive ones, or to confront and resolve the source of the anxiety.

Also, see emotional stability.

energy realm

biorhythmic balance

Return your natural physical, emotional and intellectual cycles to their normal wave patterns, where all forces equally contribute to wellbeing.

crystal blue fluorite, green fluorite, orange selenite

practice Your human biorhythmic cycles are determined from the day you are born. Consisting of a physical cycle of 23 days, an emotional cycle of 28 days, and an intellectual cycle of 33 days, the peak of each falling roughly at the midpoint of each cycle. This point is where you will feel the strongest in each sphere. At the lowest point, you are resting that sphere.

As each rises and falls according to pre-set intervals, there may be times when things feel out of balance. For example, a physical ebb may outweigh an emotional low. Or an intellectual high may be swamped by a simultaneous emotional peak where you feel intellectually stimulated, but end up in tears. And so forth.

Crystals work by attuning to the natural biorhythmic curves and giving energy to plump up or rest which ever one is dominating the rhythm, by stimulating or calming its natural wave.

energy amplification

Raise your ability to focus physical or mental activity on a single process.

crystal amazonite, purple fluorite, smoky quartz

practice Supercharge the energy forces being directed towards a particular activity or process. This is particularly useful when you feel there is a blockage of some kind, or that another element is dominating and preventing you from moving forward.

Think of this as narrowing focus, zoning out the external factors (noise), and concentrating on the subject or object with a laser beam like focus. For instance, a pre-occupation with a problem may be eliminated, allowing alternatives or choices to come to the foreground with clarity.

Amplification is only useful when working with crystals to focus on a specific issue or activity. When asking general questions, use energy stimulation or life balance instead.

Be aware that energy amplification may sap energy being used by other bodily processes, so should not be used over prolonged periods.

energy equilibrium

Find a state of perfect rest, both mentally and physically.

crystal blue fluorite, green fluorite, orange selenite

practice When all of the energies flowing through your body are equal in strength and pace, then you can consider yourself perfectly restful. This is not to say that you are asleep, just everything is flowing as it should and you are sustained.

However, when one or more energy flows are weak or strong you can feel a sense of disharmony, or that something is unbalanced. This can lead to illness, either physical or mental.

It is optimal for general well-being that all energy flows as it should, unhindered, and providing stimulation and healing where it is needed.

Equilibrium crystal work is also useful when combined with Chakra healing or rebalancing, aura cleansing, and pre-cognitive work.

energy stimulation

Raise your general energy level, build physical stamina and strength, and sharpen mental processes.

crystal clear quartz, smoky quartz

practice When you feel drained on either the physical or mental plane, your body or mind is generally telling you it is time for rest. However, sometimes rest time is not available or you cannot reschedule things that require higher energy levels.

Using crystals to provide short-term boosts to energy levels helps you to prosper when needed. It is important, however, to allow energy to ebb and the body/mind time to recuperate.

Energy stimulation can also be used when focusing on a particular element, allowing greater energy to flow through in a targeted way. It will make the element more intense and aid your ability to focus on its principles.

See also energy amplification and equilibrium.

kundalini energy

In healing, release inner base energy forces to amplify desired physical and mental outcomes.

crystal purple fluorite, smoky quartz

practice Kundalini energy is a primal energy flow, representing an important life force from which all other energies can draw strength. It is commonly an area of focus used in both Reiki and Yoga practices.

In crystal work, harnessing kundalini energy can be used to support concentration and is particularly useful when targeting physical ailments and mental impediments. Unlocking kundalini energy can provide a powerful path for healing to flow to the areas of focus.

life balance

Equalize mental and physical energy rhythms to where both equally contribute to your wellbeing. Help to deepen family relationships and ties.

crystal blue fluorite, green fluorite, orange selenite

practice Crystal work that targets life balance is useful when working on general wellbeing rather than specific problems.

Life balance is a good inclusion to any grid as it helps to harmonize the physical and mental focus, providing a grounding point and protective barrier.

When dealing with broken ties or family issues specifically, use life balance to create calm and open your communication channels in a positive way. This will allow a crossover between the physical and mental energy meridians such that they support each other and shield you from hurt. It will also assist in attaining a deeper understanding.

lightbody

Connect the physical body to the universe through the aura and the chakras. Intensify almost any of the higher realm crystals.

crystal kunzite, purple fluorite, sunstone

practice Imagine a beam of light that emanates from the universe, enters your body at the top and beams down through you till it is grounded into the earth. It is pure energy. From this energy you can harness all elements of the realms, drawing on it to heal, strengthen or calm what troubles you.

The lightbody is also used to transport you to the higher realms and connect with higher planes.

The energy flow of the lightbody can be impeded if the aura is unbalanced or if energy meridians are blocked. This can be alleviated by also working on aura strengthening or chakra rebalancing through a Reiki session.

rebirth

Balance energy through breathing. Find and arrange behaviors such that change can be enacted.

crystal girasol, pietersite, yellow opal

practice The simple act of breathing allows energy to flow through your body as intended by nature, delivering oxygen where needed for proper function. At birth, breathing is, of course, the very first thing you do.

When you are new, you are empty and pure, being a fertile vessel for information and from this point, you receive messages needed to conduct your life. As information is accumulated things become messy. Through the process of rebirthing, you can use energy to focus on organization, leading to a calmer life.

Include in a grid when seeking understanding or correction of behaviors. Also, can be used in breath therapies and when undertaking Tai Chi.

higher realm

angelic

Connect with influences that represent truth, innocence and purity, both external and internal.

crystal chalcedony, clinochlore

practice The pursuit of truth should not be a pursuit at all. You are born with both a purity of mind and an inability to convey falsehoods. However, age and experience also bring your ability to mask facts, convey untruths and develop mistrust.

To find truth in any situation which is confused or clouded, you must first connect with the child mind – either with your own or that of others – as it is in this angelic state that truth exists and is able to be understood. This means stepping away from your own bias, preconceptions, and judgments, and to see the issue from the pure unaffected viewpoint of the angelic mind.

Looking back to the birth of a situation may also reveal truth and purity.

ascended masters

Connect with higher beings that have transcended the physical world, beyond cyclical rebirthing and reincarnation to assist your own ascension process.

crystal goldstone, pietersite

practice Ascended Masters hold the collective wisdom of all mankind, the earth, and the universe. They reside in the higher realms, having learned everything that is possible from the physical world. They are the book of records for everything past, present, and future, and can freely and simply interpret all with purity and truth.

Connecting with Ascended Masters is often the ultimate aim of all students of ascension, but they are unable to impart all of their knowledge into your earthbound existence. There is simply no room or reason for you to know all, your journey is always a path of learning.

However, connecting with the love and warmth of an Ascended Master will give inspiration and help you to affirm your beliefs.

ascension

Seek to raise internal energy vibration levels and connect with higher beings through the central life force.

crystal hypersthene

practice Before attempting to attune to higher beings, you will benefit with some work on balancing energies using such tools as Reiki, Yoga or crystal therapy. It is only when energy is restful that you can make connections to most things in the higher realm, particular when you are trying to ascend.

Ascension can mean making connections with either past beings (such as ancestors) or those beings that are only ethereal and have never resided in the physical world. Most are omnipresent, however, they will only come forth when your beliefs are strong and your energies are flowing freely.

Higher beings seldom provide distinct answers. However, they will provide guidance, assisting you to find answers that you can implement in your own plane.

astral travel

Assist projection into the astral planes while you are sleeping, meditating or daydreaming. Gain greater ease of transcendence and recollection of travels.

crystal dumortierite, nuummite

practice Allowing your soul to travel to places that exist beyond your physical world can enable you to experience greater knowledge and access information that is both ancient and prophetic. It is a profound and deeply meditative experience.

In the higher realms, all things are known. This does not mean that you can access all – you are only open to knowledge that will assist you in the physical world. However, projecting your soul into the astral plane can unveil messages and affirm your beliefs that things exist beyond the here and now.

Occasional practice of astral projection will open you to the formation of new ideas, and knowledge that you are not bound by the status quo. From this, you can imagine profound change.

Hold a keepsake during meditation. Place under your pillow while sleeping.

awakening

Connect with beings on a higher plane such as ascended masters, devas or spirit guides. Develop your ability to channel.

crystal moss agate, pyrite

practice You may feel a strong connection to a particular thing or being for reasons unknown. It is as if you are being somehow guided by a spirit in another dimension. Often this can be a friend, a relative or lost loved one, or just a particular thing you are inexplicably drawn to.

To further the bond with those higher realm influences, your focus must be attuned to them such that you can be awakened on a spiritual level. Once awakened, you can provide a channel, or lightbody, through which they can travel to you, or you can travel to them.

Awakening the channels to the higher realm beings is a powerful experience. In some respects, you are giving yourself to the greatest unknown.

aura cleansing

Strengthen all or part of your body's energy aura to gain focus or balance out any of the seven colors. For specific colors, refer to the aura color chart.

crystal agate, sodalite

practice As energy emanates from your physical body, it manifests as colors that can be seen with thermographic imaging. Each color can be read to signify your relative health on a spiritual level. Your aura will change over time – warmer colors when you are invigorated and active, and cooler colors when you are calm and at peace. At given times it is beneficial to balance your aura by introducing color to counter that which appears to be dominant.

Your aura's consistency is dependent on the ability of energy to flow through your body unhindered - providing stimulation to auras that are sluggish and healing to those that are under stress.

Aura cleansing with crystals is benefitted by balanced chakras so can be used in conjunction with Reiki therapy.

Carry a keepsake or hold in the hand during meditation. Use a crystal related to a specific color spectrum in a grid when working on a particular area of the aura.

blessings

Connect with or seek guidance from religious saints, angels or from God.

crystal white selenite

practice In theology, there is a belief in a supreme being of some sort. This being represents the purest of beings, speaking only truth and imparting wisdom to assist daily life.

For followers of traditional religions, the supreme being exists in the higher realms, although their gospel is tangibly set in the physical world. This is often set in book form which acts as the lightbody connection to the supreme being. It is more demonstrable and less transient, while the same personal interpretations and interactions are still available to you.

When connecting with guides, you can interpret their guidance with reference to the written words. This will keep you grounded and help to constrain the guidance to something that is actionable and explainable. Your spirituality becomes more practical and easier to manage.

It is not necessarily the message received from the higher realm that is important as the message already exists in the gospels. What becomes important is the connection itself.

celestial

Attune with elements or ideas associated with planets or astrological bodies.

crystal vulcanite

practice For followers of astrology, planetary alignments on any given day affect your daily life, providing both positive and negative influence. You know that the earth is subject to all kinds of influence from things like the sun and the moon. It yet remains beyond science to know the effects of all celestial bodies simply because we are not yet able to examine them in close detail.

To find out how celestial bodies are influencing you, or to draw on the power of a favored planet, deflecting others and so on, choose crystals according to your astrological stone, the currently visible planets or the astrological sign of the current month.

Astrological crystals can also be used to add more energy to particular elements in any crystal grid. See the astrological crystals chart. Include in a grid when working on a specific problem or use to support another crystal where information is sought. Useful when balancing negative energy present in the astrological system.

christ consciousness

Connect with the Light of Christ above the physical world.

crystal sardonyx

practice The definition of the Light of Christ varies among Christian religions, however, a common understanding is that it represents the divine and pure light of God.

When used by lightworkers following Christian faith, opening a channel to the Light of Christ can invoke a more powerful and deeper spiritual experience.

In crystal work, it will invigorate energy, cleanse it of negativity and assist with any higher realm communication. Finding focus will also assist when any question of faith or belief arises, enabling you to "see through the darkness".

cord cutting

Assist with calling the Ascended Masters or religious figures to help break attachments to negative influences. Also, help to give problems to the universe (letting go).

crystal jadeite

practice When you recognize a negative influence is having a profound effect on your life, be it a person, an event or a state of mind – you have reached the first level of freedom in your understanding and your ability to let it go.

While it may not be possible to alter or reverse the source of the negativity itself, you are able to break its influence with conscious effort, especially if you can narrow your focus to both sides of the question: Where is the negativity coming from and how is it affecting me?

There are many remedies for cutting your ties to negative influence. A crystal representing the opposing element may be useful. For example, if a person causes you pain, give them a crystal of healing and carry a crystal of happiness yourself.

You can also ceremoniously bury (commit back to the earth) a crystal that represents the negative attachment.

devas

Connect with the Devas on the higher ascended devic plane to receive guidance and enlightenment.

crystal white selenite

practice Of all the beings available to you in the higher realm, devic energies represent the greatest unknown. From fairies to dragons, the realm of the Devas is wise and yet playful, both quiet and energetic, each distinct in its own characteristics. These creatures govern the natural world and are duty bound to take care of the earth and all of its inhabitants.

When connecting with Devas, you may feel childlike, innocent and yet full of knowledge. Some devic influence can leave you mournful and sad. All Devas have something to offer. They play with your energy as though discovering a new path to adventure - an adventure they wish to take you on.

Devic energies do not give up their wisdom easily, and patience is needed. Be open to the many facets and bask in their energy.

dreams

Seek to find solutions or work through issues while dreaming during sleep or daydreaming. Be guided on how to interpret a dream as it relates to life events or situations.

crystal nuummite, optical calcite

practice Dreams serve to assist you with processing the many messages and experiences you will receive in your life. When you are fully asleep, your mind gets to work, categorizing, filing - making sense. Dreams also signal change and help you to retrieve information in order to prepare.

Consider dreaming as being like a computer reboot. The filing system is rearranged to make room for new information and store information as memories. It addresses conflicting information and assesses what is stored in terms of whether it needs to be retained at all. Things that make you feel good, you'll tend to keep. Things that make you feel bad require further examination as to whether there is any information that may help you in the future.

To retain mental health, you must allow yourself to dream often, and preferably unhindered by drugs of any kind. Vivid dreams (that can be recalled in consciousness) signal a memory that is confused, not yet having a clear purpose. There is much to be learned from dreams.

earthbound spirits

Communicate with spirits that have left the physical body but have not transcended physical realm. These may be angels or ghosts.

crystal chalcedony, moss agate

practice As spirits pass from earth to the next world, some may be caught, unwilling or unable to transcend. Are there issues unresolved? Are there messages to give to the living?

Some may wish to act as spirit guides to the living and behave in a beneficial way, while others may demonstrate malevolence as a way of drawing attention to unresolved issues. Either way, their depleted energy causes them to remain stuck. They may scare you, but they can't harm you.

In mediumship, connecting with "the dead" can provide a valued contribution to healing, especially when grief is so profound as to have stuck the grieving firmly in stasis, unable to move forward. Connecting with earthbound spirits requires open channels, so will also be benefitted by working on energy balances. When working with potentially malevolent spirits, combine with crystals from the protective realm.

etheric body

Connect with the body of light that exists outside the aura between the physical body and the higher realm. This area is said to be truthful and pure.

crystal optical calcite, pyrite

practice Beyond the aura, the etheric body is the body of light that exists between the aura and the higher realms. It is in this light that exists all truth in its purest form. As you pass into and through this light, you are cleansed of all the negative traits and influences you carry with you.

When searching for truth you must see beyond your prejudices and assumptions. By exposing yourself to the pure light of the etheric body, truth can be revealed.

The etheric body cannot provide you with new ideas or new information. It is merely the light of revelation as nothing can exist in this realm that is deceptive or untrue. Use the etheric body when a situation is unclear or misunderstood.

goddesses

Seek guidance from the female goddesses existing in the chosen theism or religion. Help to develop femininity and grace.

crystal red jasper

practice The female influence governs your creativity and grace, as well as your feminine traits. It helps you to love in a manner that is filled with light. The female goddesses guide you in separating passion and lust from caring and nurturing, the latter assisting you to love all things unconditionally.

Goddesses will also help you to conduct your life with grace, calming the turbulence and smoothing rough edges such that your creativity can flow freely and unimpeded.

In developing feminine influences, you are able to view situations and events in a more accepting way.

inner child

Connect with the lower self to understand how behaviors learned (or not), in early life affect today's behaviors. It can also assist when ideas and mental attitudes have not yet matured or seem misunderstood.

crystal lapis lazuli

practice Where there are issues suspected to originate from childhood experiences or immature, unrealized emotions (both positive and negative), connecting with your lower self can help you to understand how these experiences impact you today.

In negative experiences, you can often carry these through your life, keeping you in a victim like state. If this is the case, inner child crystal work should include elements that deal with letting go or cutting cords.

In recapturing positive experiences, including happy memories, and those that represent innocence, include inner child crystal work with elements that deal with the past.

karma

Further your understanding of how actions can affect future paths. Assist in decision making.

crystal sardonyx, vulcanite

practice Everything you do represents an action of some kind, even if it is the act of doing nothing much. The focus of the action, and the way you approach it is called karma.

Karma is a reflective outward projection. You've heard of bad karma, which is when an action has a negative impact on someone or something. To transform bad karma into positivity requires you to make a conscious decision to do so, being mindful of how your actions will influence others.

In projecting positive karma, you can influence how you receive karma. If you want an action of your own doing to bear results in a positive way, either by influencing some external situation or by having that external situation then reflect back positivity. Some consideration of your own behavioral karma is key.

knowledge

Increase your ability to learn and gain experience through heightened knowledge.

crystal sardonyx

practice When studying, this element can be useful to facilitate understanding, making things easier to learn, retain and relate. It also enables you to be more receptive to new information.

The knowledge that is gained from experience rather than study, can become more relevant. You can open yourself to the messages contained therein, and help yourself to commit experience to memory in a positive way.

When working on specific issues, this element can be used to enable you to draw on past experience or learning to help solve current or future issues.

metaphysics

Answer questions or gain some understanding of ideas that cannot be easily explained or proven with conventional reasoning.

crystal optical calcite

practice Connecting with the higher realms helps to develop philosophical ideas. Here greater questions can be answered such as "what is my life purpose?" It also assists you to become more accepting and willing to exchange ideas in a non-judgmental way.

In use, this element assists when you are trying to communicate new ways of thinking, especially when you think that doing so may cause controversy or upset.

mother earth

Connect with the earth mother goddess to strengthen bonds to nature and amplify the female (creative) side of your personality and mind.

crystal pietersite, red jasper, tiger's eye

practice Grace and nurturing are often the first things to fall when your life become unbalanced. In these times you can call upon the earth mother to ground you and bring you back to calm. There is a lightness, if not a degree of fragility which will often counterbalance the things that weigh on you.

The earth mother represents all things female, including fertility and growth. Where there are motherhood concerns, connecting with the earth mother Goddess may assist.

oversoul

Connect with a side of the soul that exists between the physical being and the higher self.

crystal chalcedony, goldstone

practice The oversoul has knowledge of both your worldly state (imperfect) and the higher self which is the embodiment of your creator (perfect).

When personality or behavioral problems persist, reaching out to the oversoul may give insights to understand or correct traits, or interpret them in a new way. With insights, you are able to correct issues, make changes and move forward.

Hold a keepsake during meditation or use in a grid when seeking to understand. Useful in the virtuous realm when trying to understand or correct a personal trait.

reincarnate

Assist when trying to change a path or move forward with new ideas and opportunities.

crystal pyrite, yellow opal

practice Reincarnation in crystal work relates to the physical world, governing invention and future outcomes of change that are unknown or unpredictable. It enables you to examine your life and see areas where you are stuck.

It helps you to embrace change. This could be as simple as changing jobs, moving house or entering a new relationship. In drawing on higher realm elements, you can open yourself to influences that will guide you through transformation. It helps you to not dwell on the past and to understand that a positive approach means moving toward something, rather than moving away from something else.

Include in a grid when working on some aspect of change. Use with a manifestation stone.

spirit guardians

Assist calling any or all guardian spirits, including spirit guides, ascended angels, or gods and goddesses.

crystal black onyx, moss agate, tiger's eye

practice With any therapy that seeks to heal the mind or body, you can draw on beings in the higher realms to provide a powerful source of guardian energy. Guardian spirits are here to both protect you and guide you while providing information that can assist you in your earthbound life.

Spirit guardianship comes in two forms. The first is to guard you against harm from negative influences in the physical world by providing you with clear directions and paths. The second is to keep safe the wisdom they hold, such that you can draw on them to guide you in your journey in a positive way.

Connecting with any higher being should not be just a pursuit of answers. These you must find yourself as you will have a different purpose to everyone else. However, with conscious connection and acknowledgment of your higher guardians, you can access their wisdom to provide a safe way forward.

Carry a keepsake when visiting places where spirits are believed to reside for better connection to their energy.

spirit guides

Ask for spirit guides to assist with specific issues.

crystal black onyx, clinochlore

practice Calling your spirit guides helps you to confront issues that cause you pain, fear or uncertainty. With access to the higher realm spirits, you can receive the courage to face issues head on. You can also undertake challenges free of apprehension.

Spirit guides are here to help you but to receive their guidance you must first ask for it. It is best to use this element without expectation of a specific answer – rather be open to any kind of answer. This way you can be more open and responsive to guidance received.

time travel

As per astral travel or soul flight where the desire is to gain insights into the past or future worlds.

crystal dumortierite, nuummite

practice Allowing your soul to travel to places that exist beyond your physical world can enable you to experience greater knowledge and access information that is both ancient and prophetic. It is a profound and deeply meditative experience. In time travel you can specifically project into the past or the future.

In the higher realms, all things are known. This does not mean that you can access all – you are only open to knowledge that will assist you in the physical world. However, projecting your soul into the astral plane can unveil messages and affirm your beliefs that things exist beyond the here and now.

Using astral traveling with a focus on the future opens you to the formation of new ideas, and knowledge that you are not bound by the status quo.

Using astral traveling with a focus on the past assists your understanding of present day issues and affirms your sense of belonging.

vibration

Seek to connect with other people or entities on a higher level or with deeper meaning. Also, see ascension.

crystal amethyst

practice In a human sense, accessing the energy vibrations of crystals can help you to attune to the vibrations of others. It helps you to understand their behaviors through their emanating energy. It may be as simple as saying "I get you", or developing a deeper feeling of empathy.

Vibrating crystal light can also be used to pass good energy to souls that are weakened or dispirited. Alternatively, you can access the positive vibrations of external influences to strengthen your own vibration fields.

You can also attune to the vibrations of objects even when the object appears inert.

material realm

fortune

Attract financial abundance or stability.

crystal aventurine, chrysoprase, cinnabarite

practice This element specifically deals with money. After love, it is perhaps the most widely used element of all.

As you move forward, accumulating possessions and running your affairs, your need for financial abundance and stability grows as it is typically associated with the pleasurable activities needed to make your life enjoyable. However, you risk becoming single-minded in its pursuit. It is wise to disconnect fortune with other specific elements as you may position yourself to sacrifice one for the other.

The definition of financial abundance will be different for each person, so first, determine what it looks like for you. Is it "I just want to be able to pay my bills on time" or is it "I want to be a millionaire." Or somewhere in between? Stability can also be useful in times of temporary economic stress.

good luck

Attract a certain positive outcome, acquisition or gain where chance is a factor.

crystal citrine

practice Anything that involves chance indicates there are many possible outcomes, the two most common being simply winning or losing. Luck is inherent in anything that is some sort of competition, and that competition may be with other people vying for the same outcome, or with yourself where a specific outcome is desired. It is just one of a number of possibilities.

In this instance, attracting good luck is for a specific "prize" in a specific event or situation. For more general positive outcomes that are not specific, or to feel generally fortunate, combine with other elements to widen the sphere.

manifestation

Bring something that is desired to the foreground or view, or into actual reality.

crystal clear quartz

practice There are many ways to work on manifestation. Followers of the Laws of Attraction will attest to the outcomes when focus is placed on objects or situations of desire. Manifestation in this context allows channels to open such that your wants become a central point, with a positive view.

In practical use, with a focus on the objective, you are compelled to question your intentions. For example, if the desired outcome is a home, the affirmations "I don't want to be homeless" and "I want to live in this house" both seem to apply. However, the first does not focus on a specific positive outcome as it is general and undefined. The second allows you to be specific.

In crystal use, manifestation can be combined with many other crystals to provide clarity and visualization.

philanthropy

Receive guidance on giving or receiving financial or material gifts.

crystal aventurine

practice Philanthropy governs both money and material things that you perceive to have value in some form. With material items, the value may not necessarily be monetary, however, considered beneficial.

In this case, chance is not a factor, but rather a conscious and directed decision. Therefore, the act of giving or receiving things of value in the form of gifts – where no expectation of repayment is attached – must come with the right intent.

To develop firm intentions, you can use crystals to focus your thoughts and influence the outcome in a positive way.

prosperity

Ask for enduring success in a particular endeavor or in financial areas.

crystal aventurine, chrysoprase, cinnabarite

practice Today, prosperity is often associated just with wealth, however, it can also govern health and well-being. In times past, the term prosperity was used to describe a period of abundance or when things were thriving and doing well. In crystal work, you can focus on prosperity to foster growth and success in all manner of endeavors. It is enduring.

In this focus, it may be something such as doing well in school or helping your career, friendships, and physical health. Prosperity is also aligned with your ability to adapt and change. If you are stuck you cannot move forward, things cannot grow. By focusing on prosperity you are opening yourself to change such that your endeavors can be prosperous, giving you the outcomes that lead to a full and enriched life.

meditation realm

channeling

Clear your mind such that suggestion or questioning is unimpeded by everyday thoughts.

crystal goldstone

practice Usually, trance states open you to the powers of suggestion from either influence in the physical world, such as experienced in hypnosis sessions, or from the ethereal world such as experienced in channeling. From both, you can receive healing in a deeply physical way through suggestion.

In crystal work, using the light and energy that comes with being in their presence, helps to clear the mind.

daydreams

Achieve a state where pleasant thoughts preoccupy your mind while awake.

crystal howlite, nuummite

practice Daydreaming helps you to visualize your hopes and ideals. Unlike strict meditation, in daydreaming you allow your mind to be filled with thoughts. In this state, your imagination comes to the foreground and you can create - imagining how you would like your life to be, events to occur or situations to arise. You can picture yourself within those images.

At times, daydreaming can also help to organize and provide clarity, as in this element you can eliminate the things that worry or concern you and visualize life without them. It is in this visualization that you can create your ideal world and then move toward bringing it into reality.

Wear as jewelry or hold as a keepsake, especially while daydreaming. Include in a grid when asking for a specific outcome or use to support other crystals involved in visualizing an ideal outcome.

meditation

visualisation

Achieve a state where the mind is free of thoughts and only conscious of breath while awake.

crystal howlite, nuummite

practice Meditation helps to clear your mind and completely take your body to a rested state. It helps you to balance energy flows and clear blockages without consciously working on doing so.

Meditation allows your mind and body to attune to the rhythm as nature intended. As you focus on breath only, you are conscious only of the fact that you are aware. This delivers pranic healing as both the mind and body are allowed to rest, rebalance and recuperate.

With the realization that this state is possible (enlightenment), mediation becomes a profoundly healing experience.

Develop and ease mental images during a healing session. Visualize things that "can be".

crystal scolecite

practice Visualization is closely connected to daydreaming, however, in this element, you can narrow your focus to a single point rather than the random thoughts of daydreams. It is singular, where you can imagine a distinct situation in real terms.

Visualization is useful when paired with many other elements, especially where change is sought.

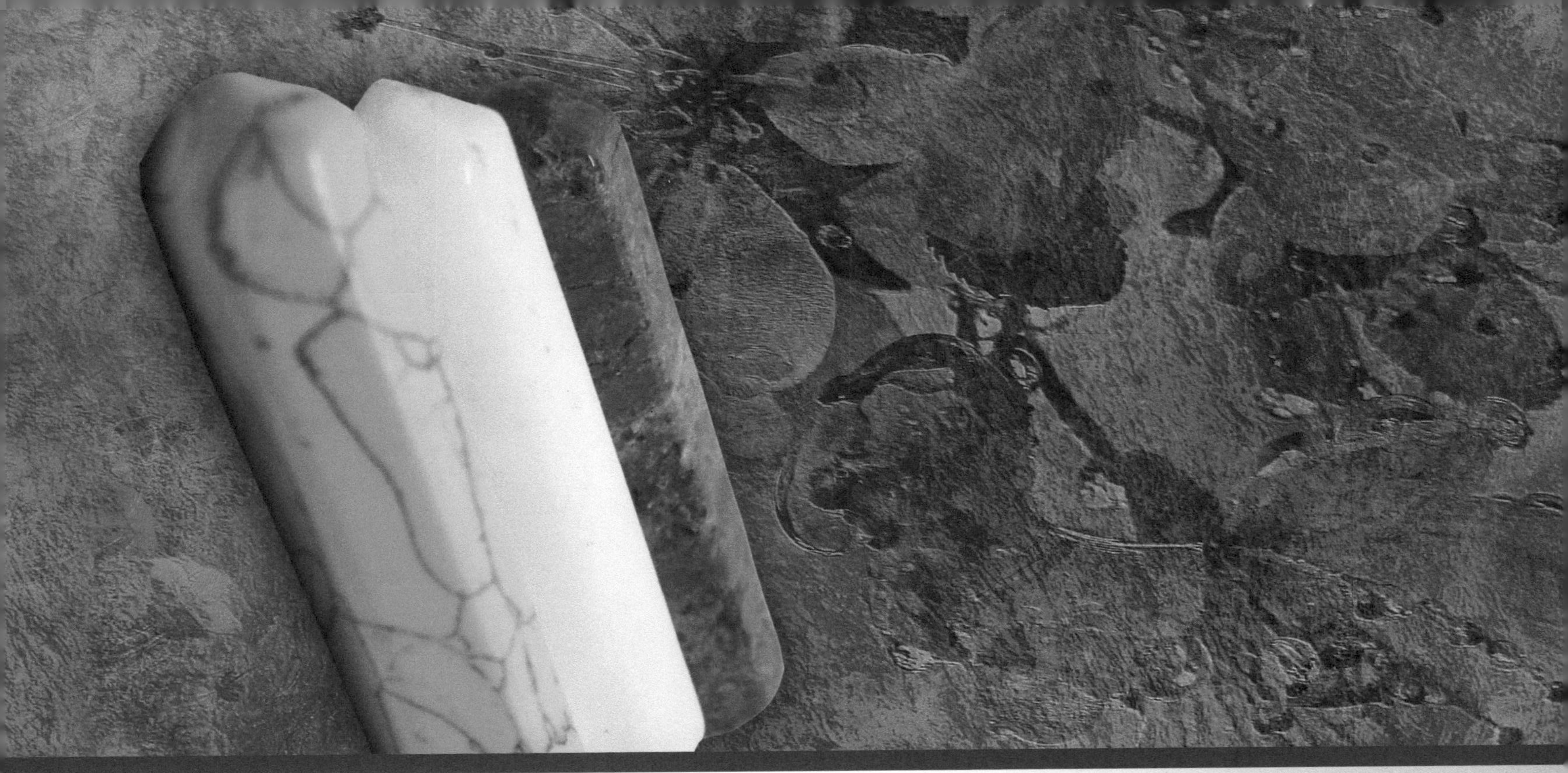

physical realm

blood flow

Raise or condition the circulation of energy through the blood system to assist endurance and recovery.

crystal cobalt aura, kyanite, turquoise

practice When practicing healing with crystals, you can draw on their energy to positively move healing throughout the body. As blood carries oxygen, nutrients, and medicines as needed, so it carries energy too.

When your practices positively charge that energy you can help the body to both regenerate and recover.

Wear as jewelry or place on the body during healing sessions. Include in a grid when working on a specific problem that requires energy to flow through the body.

bones

Assist relief of bone and joint related pain such as arthritis or rheumatism.

crystal cobalt aura, garnet, turquoise

practice Supporting the skeletal system, especially when bones are broken or compromised and particularly as you age, is fundamental to function in your daily life. Simple movement can occasionally be impeded, often causing further degeneration.

While traditional medicines, natural remedies, and an active lifestyle can assist, pain caused by compromised bone structures will draw focus.

In this case, crystals will help to shift the focus away from the pain, toward the remedies, which will, in turn, compel you to take positive action.

general health

Promote a healthy diet and lifestyle. Assist recovery from minor illness. Focus on goals related to physical activity.

crystal garnet, turquoise

practice The power of positive thought has been well documented in its ability to contribute to your general health and to assist with recovery from illness.

As energy flows carry positivity, rehabilitation is aided when you focus on increasing your energy levels and dispelling negative influences.

Wear as jewelry or hold as a keepsake. Place in the corners of the home or work environment especially where exposure to toxicity is prevalent. Include in a beacon.

immunity

Support a healthy diet designed to assist recovery after illness or help prevent illness. Support the thymus function during growth phases, particularly in adolescence. Assist with energy flows through the lymphatic system. Restore balance and support immunity.

crystal cobalt aura, girasol, turquoise

practice A weakened immune system will inevitably lead to health issues. This may manifest in physical, mental or spiritual problems as each tries to counter the imbalance of energy flows. While traditional medicines and remedies may be necessary to address the physical and mental issues, resultant spiritual issues are often dismissed or ignored.

In lightwork, spiritual strength is considered a key factor in illness, where both prevention and recovery will benefit from focusing on energy flows and balance.

Crystal work should strive to raise spirituality focus as a complementary healing therapy where the immune system is considered compromised.

inflammation

Assist recovery or disassociate pain from minor inflammation problems. Foster understanding of recurrent problems.

crystal cobalt aura, garnet, turquoise

practice Inflammatory diseases debilitate and are often recurrent affecting just about every organ, muscle, and bone in the body. Inflammation can also come in a spiritual sense where energy fails to flow, cumulating in mental thoughts that cause disharmony and discomfort.

Recurrent inflammation is a symptom of unresolved issues both in spirit and in mind. Issues that cause worry distract you from addressing those problems, allowing inflammation to run freely.

Working on inflammation problems, both with medications and therapies will be benefitted with meditation and calming practices that allow you to focus on issues.

metabolism

Support metabolic rate, particularly in sport or strenuous physical activity.

crystal purple fluorite, turquoise

practice To provide support during physical activity, and where needed, raise the metabolic rate to support active weight goals, aid digestion and assist dealing with food intolerances.

In crystal work, focus on harnessing the energy flows during activity to assist with power, endurance, and recovery.

protection realm

aura strengthening

Use in conjunction with aura cleansing when managing changes or when a particular aura color is weak. For specific colors, refer to the aura color chart.

crystal agate, rhodochrosite, sunstone

practice A healthy aura may provide protection against unhealthy or negative influences and can act as a barrier to potential external threats.

Aura strengthening is useful when you feel overcome with work or when events in your life seem chaotic and appear to be "dragging you down" for reasons beyond your control.

To strengthen your aura, work with crystals that represent the specific colors. In a grid, always use crystals related to specific colors when working on a particular area of the aura. In barrier building, use all colors in their radiating positions.

ceremonial stability

Protect from negative influences during ritual or ceremonial activities.

crystal fuchsite, hematite, rhodochrosite, unakite

practice In any kind of spiritual ritual, you can invoke the potential for negative influences to enter your world or practice, especially as your awareness and sensitivity to the various elements increases. There is always scope for things to happen during ceremonies that were unintended. Good and bad!

To maintain a calm, nurturing and peaceful environment, keep a stability crystal near the earth during grid work, or wear as jewelry when participating in group sessions.

May also be useful in everyday situations that feel threatening or potentially uncomfortable.

Include in a grid to provide clear channels especially when negative influences may be anticipated.

grounding

Connect with the earth to dispel excess energy or absorb negative energy.

crystal hematite, scolecite, tiger's eye

practice At times you can become filled with excess energy that can lead you to difficulties, creating chaos and discomfort where you want peace and calm. This is especially true when using crystals to channel light into energy and connect with the elements, particularly those in the higher realm.

Grounding crystals provide a return path for positive energy, clearing and calming the energy flow.

When crystal work is intense, or when it signals profound change, use a grounding crystal to return the balance back into the real world. In grids, place a grounding crystal in the soul position after clearing the grid, and let it sit for some time.

manifested entities

Protect from negative entities entering the crystal ritual or help banish manifested influences from the energy sphere. Remove unwanted or stubborn blockages.

crystal carnelian, fuchsite, rhodochrosite, unakite

practice In any spiritual ritual, you open yourself to the presence of unwanted entities. In some respects, this is a manifest of fear as such entities are drawn to this emotion.

A manifested entity may appear as a spirit from the higher realm but can also persist as a memory of someone or an experience that has caused you pain or discomfort in the past. These represent blockages or barriers along your spiritual path.

In the latter case, there is a remaining issue to be addressed before you can move forward.

negativity

Assist in processing and transforming negative energy in order to reflect positivity back into the physical world.

crystal rhodonite, serpentine

practice Although you like to live in a positive world, there will always be times when negativity surrounds you, either emanating from other people or through circumstance.

You may be able to do very little to alter the source of the negativity, however, you can do a lot to transform that energy into something that impacts you positively. You can also choose to ignore it and let it just pass over.

Negativity is not all bad. It is a very grounding element as it gives insight into what can be, and a means for comparing the state of your life.

Repelling negativity does not mean avoiding it, as within there are things to be learned. If you view negativity this way – as something to be transformed – your lightwork activities are enriched and fruitful.

psychic attack

Protect against psychic attack being projected by others, both from the physical and spiritual world.

crystal fuchsite, rhodochrosite, unakite

practice There are some who project negativity in an apparently targeted, often malevolent manner. To a lightworker, it feels very singular and personal. It may cause you to feel judged and to possibly question your beliefs. An attack can cause blockages in your own spiritual path.

It's easy to dismiss these projections as coming from a place that is dark and unenlightened. In most cases this is true, nonetheless, you may still feel the effects in a very profound way.

To protect yourself from psychic attack, it is best to remain calm and quiet. Allow the attack to pass over you without leaving a negative imprint.

psychic vampirism

Protect against the drain of pranic energy caused when in the presence of a psychic vampire.

crystal fuchsite, rhodochrosite, unakite

practice You may have encountered psychic vampires occasionally – those who seemingly dampen energy or completely drain you of your spiritual lightness. They can be real people – often emotionally or socially absent, likely denying spirituality on every level. Or they can be celestial beings encountered in the non-physical world. In both cases, it causes you to feel saddened or disconnected.

To protect against the drain caused by a psychic vampire, you must first feel sympathy for their state – their path to enlightenment is blocked or has not yet begun. You must also recognize that it is not your place to start that journey for them. You can only shield yourself from their negative influence.

Use these crystals to form a barrier or to absorb negativity and always cleanse these crystals after use.

shamanic ritual

Assist in repelling or overcoming malevolent spirits during shamanic rituals.

crystal hematite, rhodochrosite, unakite

practice In the tradition of shamanic practice, a Shaman invites both benevolent and malevolent spirits to enter the world and often what is channeled cannot be chosen by the Shaman.

To enable connection to the more positive spirits and ward off the negative influences, especially those that seek to harm, you must be able to recognize one from the other, while acknowledging that each has a potential purpose or message to convey.

In using crystals, you can help to negate any potential for harm caused by the invocation of negative beings, while also providing them a path through which to travel to and from this world.

Wear as jewelry or hold as a keepsake while undertaking shamanic rituals. Place in a doorway or near a fire to provide a departure path.

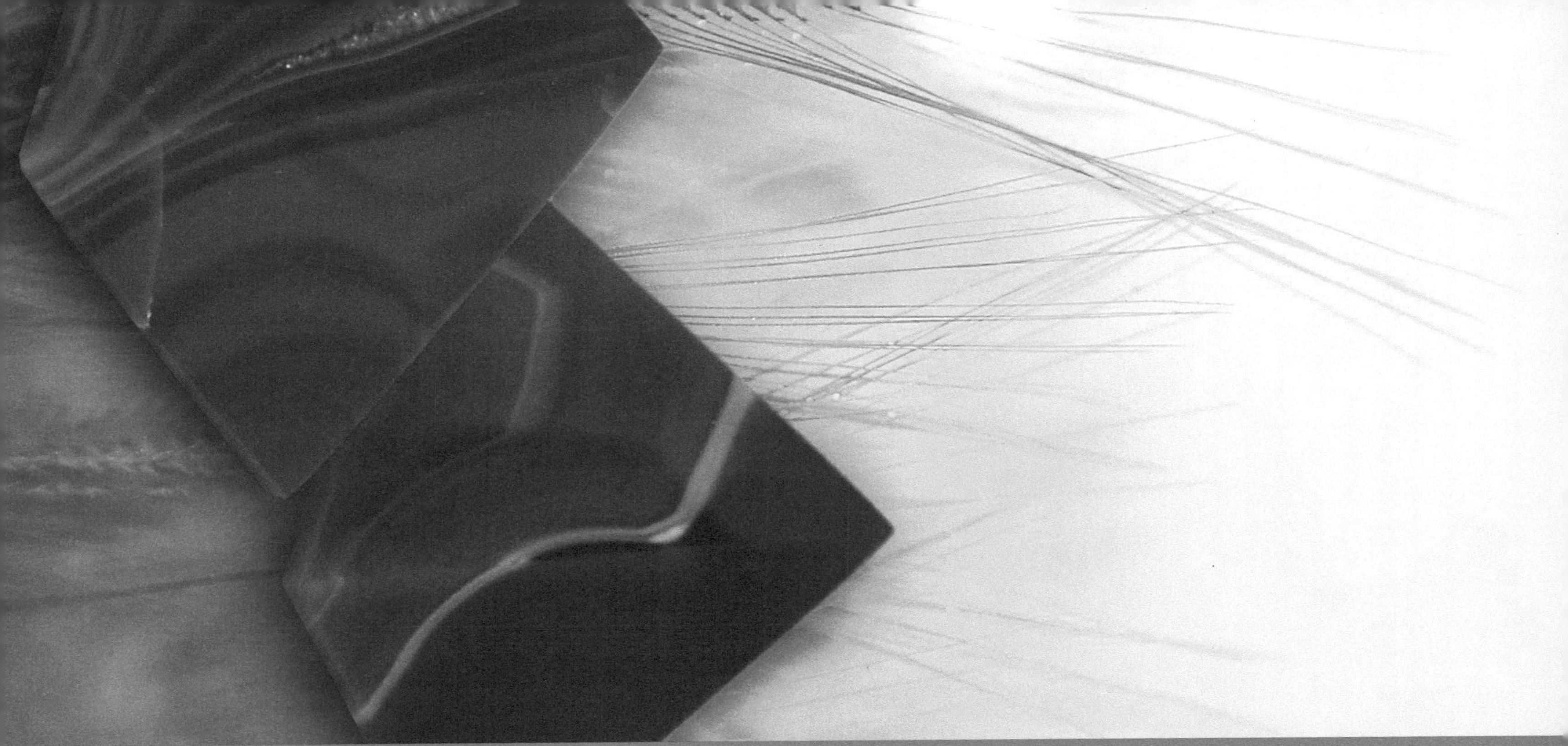

psychic realm

clairaudience

Assist in the development of the aural (sound and music) sense used in psychic practice.

crystal aquamarine

practice Messages from the spirit world or higher realms that are received as sounds indicate a clairaudient ability. This is perhaps one of the most common of the psychic abilities seen in mediumship today, particular when receiving communications from those that have passed from the physical world.

In developing clairaudience, you can draw on the energy that resonates in the physical world. This is best seen in the form of music, but can also come from sources such as Tibetan chimes, drums, chants and sounds of nature.

When working with crystals to develop clear messages, you can focus on the sounds around you and tune yourself to their rhythm. In doing so you hear the notes, pitch, and tone using the energy from the crystals to heighten your auditory channels.

Position as a soul stone in a grid for the specific purpose of developing clairaudience, or as a supporting crystal when seeking clear messages from other elements. Hold a keepsake during psychic activities or when practicing mediumship.

clairsentience

Assist in the development of the touch senses in psychic practice, particularly during psychometry practice.

crystal aquamarine

practice A clairsentient ability works in two ways. Firstly, by touching an object you may reveal its past and gather messages from the history of that object in a way that relates to the current physical world. Secondly, an object may become a channel where knowledge simply passes through, emanating from either the higher realms or past souls.

In mediumship, use the energy of the crystal held in one hand while touching the object with the other, creating a light channel between the two.

Position as a soul stone in a grid for the specific purpose of developing clairsentience. Hold a keepsake during psychic activities or psychometric readings.

clairvoyance

Assist in the development of the vision senses in psychic practice where perception is not physically based.

crystal aquamarine

practice Clairvoyant messages can present to you as either surreal or real images, and can come as premonitions (future events) or as expositions (past events). In all cases, they must be clear visual images which are distinct from mere memories of the viewer.

Clairvoyant images are received without meaning, seemingly random and obtuse. They may be persistent or fleeting, influenced by a person or object. It is the up to the clairvoyant to interpret these images in a meaningful way, without judgment or prejudicial ideas.

In this psychic medium, trusting instinct is key as it is usual the first image that is most accurate - before it has been rationalized. Crystal work will help you to open clairvoyant channels, receive clear images and describe those images exactly as they present.

Position as a soul stone in a grid for the specific purpose of developing clairvoyance. Wear as jewelry or carry a keepsake during psychic activities or tarot readings and during remote readings.

clairalience

Assist in the development of the olfactory senses (smell) in psychic practice.

crystal aquamarine

practice Clairalient sense is usually associated with some sort of warning, therefore it is usually precognitive, providing guidance to future events. A simple example would be smelling smoke where no fire exists, as a premonition of a future blaze.

In a guiding sense, you may also sense aromas that you associate with a particular person, signaling that person is spiritually present in your current plane. An aroma may also help to jog a memory such that you can retrieve information that is needed to help you in the present moment. Clairalient messages may be presented as a warning or as a comfort in a situation which is about to occur.

To develop clairalient senses, crystal work will help you to open clairalient channels and understand the messages they carry.

Position as a soul stone in a grid for the specific purpose of developing clairalience. Carry a keepsake during psychic activities or when practicing clairalience.

claircognizance

Assist in the development of the intuitive senses in psychic practice.

crystal aquamarine

practice In mediumship, claircognizance is perhaps the most widely practiced while often being the least understood. Such ability is often described as just good intuition.

Many people with claircognizant abilities never recognize their talent. Their eventual realization may be as profound as the knowledgeable thoughts they seemingly get from nowhere! It does not mean they can recite facts or display great general knowledge – it's just they appear to understand things at a higher level, in a way that seems completely logical.

As an intuitive sense, claircognizance means you know something to be true without having experience of the matter. It is better described as a deeply profound sense of knowing, but for reasons unknown.

In developing a claircognizant sense, you are led to trust your instincts without getting hung up on the sound reasoning, and in this respect, you focus on acceptance of the greater unknown. In crystal work, acknowledging there are things unknown opens you to learning. Acceptance of your beliefs is key and with this, you can find answers or reasons that lead to greater understanding.

mediumship

Assist in the development of ability to receive messages from the spiritual world.

crystal aquamarine, goldstone, sardonyx

practice Calling on spirits to deliver messages on command is challenging for anyone practicing mediumship. It requires intense focus while simultaneously being relaxed, allowing energy to flow unimpeded.

Opening channels of light to the spirit world can be enhanced by working on any of the higher realm elements that pertain to light, in combination with any of the psychic "clairs" – whichever way you choose to receive messages. As such, the mediumship stones will always complement other stones relating to the psychic realm.

When working with crystals in mediumship, where messaging is for other people, it is best for the medium's crystal to be attuned to the medium rather than the individual for whom the messages are intended.

Position as a soul stone in a grid for the specific purpose of developing mediumship or use to support other psychic elements. Wear as jewelry or carry a keepsake when in practice.

See also awareness and consciousness.

precognition

Assist in the development of ability to foresee future events or understand the meaning of premonitions.

crystal aquamarine

practice Premonitions usually come without effort or warning. They can feel quite real and probable. Like clairvoyant images, precognitive visions seem to be real events but in a precognitive sense, always relating to future events.

Premonitions often occur when the energy flows are heated and rapid, however, the visual image will be retained long after the energy flow cools and returns to normal. It is for this reason that premonitions are often reported during sleep, especially when the sleeping environment is warm to hot.

To understand the meaning of premonitions, combine work with crystals in the energy realm.

Position a soul stone in a grid for the specific purpose of developing precognition.

psychic energy

Assist in raising the mental energy required for psychic practice.

crystal amethyst

practice In all of the psychic elements, at times the energy required to form message channels may feel weak or compromised with negative energy.

To strengthen and clear energy paths in psychic practice, increasing the energy will both speed the flow of information and allow messages to become clear and unjumbled.

Position a soul stone in a grid for the specific purpose of raising or toning energy in the psychic plane.

telepathy

Assist in opening channels for sending and receiving information intuitively and telepathically.

crystal aquamarine

practice While most of the psychic elements focus on receiving messages, telepathy seeks to form a two-way path between the medium and the messenger, and in the case of the messenger may be a living person or animal, or a spirit who has passed.

When working to enhance telepathic abilities, also use crystals that deal with travel and light channels.

relationship realm

bonds

Healing or fostering relationships on any level, or strengthening bonds.

crystal pink calcite, red jasper, rose quartz

practice A sense of disconnection can leave you feeling lonely and isolated. Left in this state you can become susceptible to all kinds of negative influence. As positive emotional energy needs a path of external release, you simply need to form bonds of some kind – you need something to care about.

Your "care" relationship can be with people, animals, nature or simply the things that interest you. These bonds can be on an intimate level, however, this does not determine whether a bond exists - you are free to keep boundaries and stay within your comfort zones.

Forming or strengthening bonds is dependent on you first identifying the all-important outlet for your positive energy as well as the thing you wish to bond with.

break ties

Work to release ties to people, habits, beliefs and environments that are toxic, counter-productive or negative.

crystal jadeite

practice Forming habits is easy as you usually like to repeat actions that give you some sort of pleasure. Or you may remain with things that have been constant in your life – no matter whether they convey negativity or not, or regardless of whether they no longer give you joy.

You also tie yourself to things that are familiar and comfortable as confrontation is a less attractive option. These become the furniture of life. They just exist with you because you do nothing to remove them. In this, you also adhere them to your own habit.

If a tie does not produce a positive influence, the universe is telling you it is time to let go. In order to discover and grow, you must make room.

When working with crystals, also use elements that help to visualize a future without the negative influences.

brotherhood

Connect with the male dominant personality side or bond male relationships on a personal or professional level.

crystal ametrine, mookaite, pietersite

practice The male influence governs logic and your process of undertaking tasks in an orderly manner. It also guards you against the impact of emotions and enables you to reveal practical values in relationships and objects. You can see things as they really are, rather than how you imagine them to be.

Working on brotherhood is useful in the relationship realm where you are conflicted or uncertain of the nature of the bond. It is not purely about love and can be applied in a more practical sense to all aspects of your dealings with other people or situations.

friendship

Open channels to platonic relationships or to mend broken relationships in a non-threaten or non-confrontational way. Help to connect with a twin flame.

crystal ametrine, pink calcite

practice When relationships exist beyond just associations (although not intimate), you are in the middle ground of friendship. Here you are able to feel many elements from love and caring to communication and respect.

Your view of friendship will evolve over time, representing different things at different stages of your life. Childhood friendships will be different to adulthood friendships. Often they may only be fleeting, but each plays a valuable role in your path forward, while the relationship endures.

Working on forming friendships means tapping into the energy combination of many elements, particularly those of self-awareness. In mending broken friendships you can also work on other virtuous elements such as forgiveness and acceptance.

unconditional love

Attract love without ties or fears, in a truthful and positive way. Promote the ability to give love unconditionally.

crystal rose quartz

practice Love that is unbounded and unconstrained is the purest form of dedication to people and things you hold dear in your life. There is no sense of duty, there are no reasons, and it is limitless.

Giving or receiving this kind of love is a beautiful experience and fills you with positive emotions which you can then harness to positively charge energy in everything you do.

When working on unconditional love you can ask two questions: "Why do I love?" and "What would make me love or stop me loving?" In reality, there should be no answers here. It is still love if there are, which is good in itself, but you can then understand there are conditions attached.

Unconditional love is both precious and precarious. It can be destroyed by things you cannot anticipate or by conditions that you are unaware of. In this respect, you should deeply value the joy it brings, for however long it remains.

unity

Assist in finding or attracting like-mindedness.

crystal magnesite, orange selenite, pink calcite

practice Feelings of disconnection can lead you to sit in observation of life instead of active participation, especially in your own journey. You are drawn to those that think the same as you, and to the things you like, but sometimes they seem unreachable.

In building unity you must do so in respect of your own values and views – you cannot join in just for the sake of being united. There must be something tangible you connect with.

Don't despair. If you feel you cannot connect it means you have yet to seek. This is a time to build on your own self-awareness and find what's true to you. This will lead you to unity.

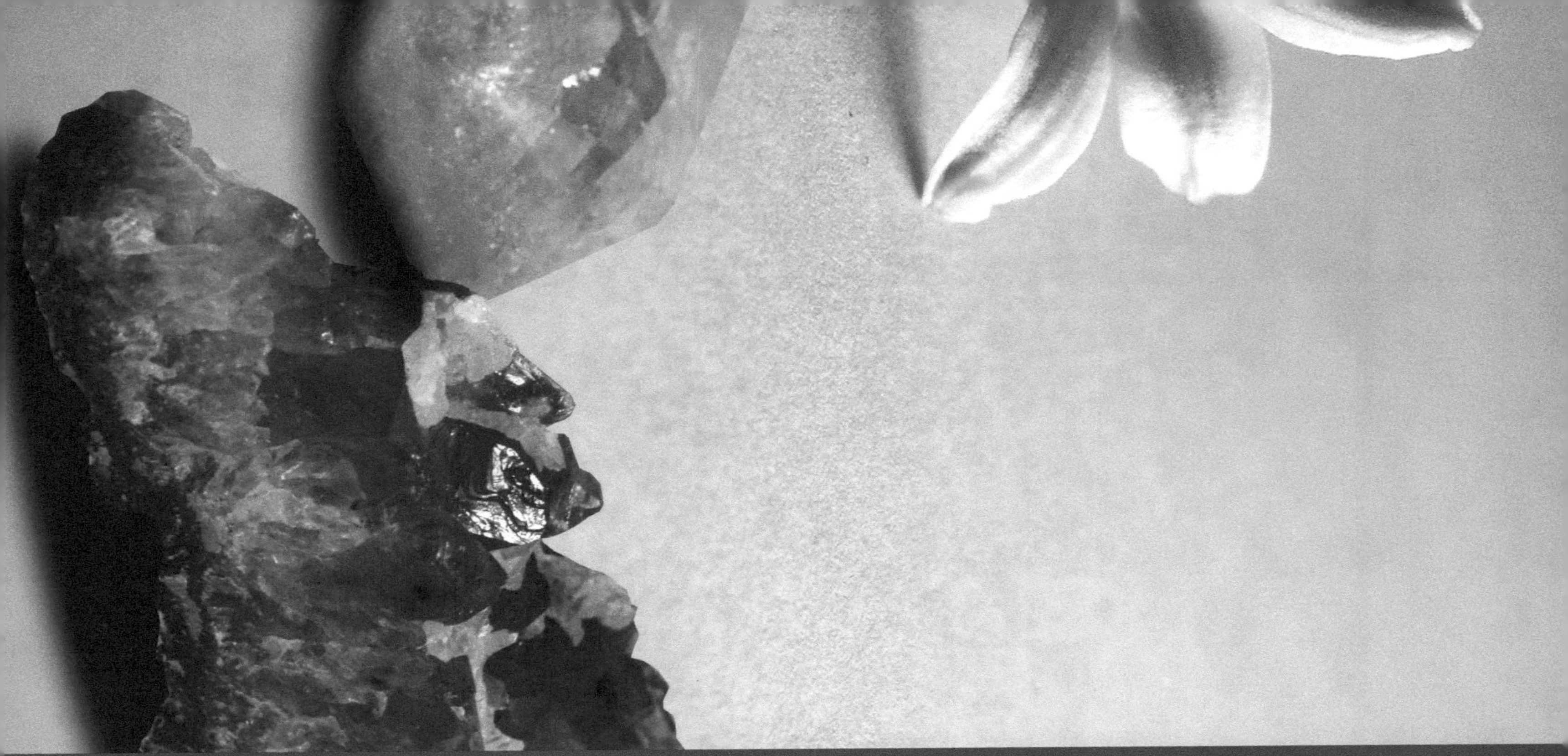

virtuous realm

acceptance

Assist in receiving an outcome to a situation or perceived problem. Have something that is given received in the light for which it is intended.

crystal pink calcite

practice Of all the virtues, acceptance is possibly the single and most vital imperative. Your acceptance of current situations, or past events, is key to releasing you from barriers and allowing you to imagine ways forward. In this imagination, you can evoke profound change.

Acceptance does not indicate agreement or complicity. It merely means that you understand how you got to where you are at. Rather than trying to change the past or to ponder how different things could have been, which is futile, you can use what you have learned to continue your journey in a positive way. Like a river, life will bend and change course over time, and there will be many whirlpools to discover. What's important is that you do not try to continually swim upstream and that you allow the river to flow.

addiction

Help to break bad or damaging habits and form or attract new habits.

crystal bronzite, snowflake obsidian

practice In most therapies designed to eradicate addictions, you are inclined to focus on the damaging sides of the habit in the hope that this will help you to avoid the behavior and change your mindset. However, to break any addiction that is having a negative impact, you also need to see your life without the addiction. To do this you can imagine beyond the addictive influence and focus on the positive outcomes.

For example, to quit drugs, you can imagine what you will do with the money or time saved or a better state of physical health. To cease obsessive compulsions you can imagine the productive time spent doing other things.

Focusing on something positive to run to, rather than something negative to run away from, will lead you to better outcomes.

allowance

Build tolerance or enable permission to behave or exist in a certain way. Free negative blockages and repel negativity.

crystal epidote, lepidolite

practice Allowance has both a positive and negative aspect and it is necessary to understand which of these you are focusing on. As a simple example, "I won't allow myself to be bullied" or "I will give myself permission to stand up for myself" are opposing sides of the same issue. The former is a negative focus whereas the latter is positive.

In working on allowance, determine the opposing views and choose to focus on the positive. Allow it "to be".

Focus on allowance can also influence how others accept you and your beliefs/actions, and how you accept the beliefs/actions of other people.

anger

Assist in dealing with issues that cause feelings of anger, or to help dispel those feelings where the situation cannot be changed.

crystal carnelian, rhodonite

practice Anger is an inward emotion that you outwardly express. Things will cause you to feel anger, it is part of being human. It has both a physical and mental effect as it builds up energy within you. This energy can bubble out, in turn affecting those around you, making you uncomfortable and disturbing your peace. Eventually, you snap.

In dealing with anger, you must deal with the energy it creates. You can learn to direct it into another activity such as a sport, housework, gardening or some such, anything that is not directly connected to the feeling of anger but rather the resulting energy. If you expel that energy in a positive way, the anger becomes just temporary.

Anger energy feeds on other energy like a lightning rod so if you become the recipient of anger you must learn not to add fuel. You must treat it quietly. That is not to become submissive but to understand it will pass.

animosity

Help to deal with feelings of hatred, jealousy, envy or dislike both given and received.

crystal rhodonite

practice Animosity is one of the most negative aspects of behavior. What can begin as just a simple dislike, can manifest into hatred, and when this happens the hatred becomes deep-seated and consuming. It is when animosity causes actions that real damage can be done.

In making the distinction between dislike and animosity you can begin to understand how it impacts your life. For example, you may dislike carrots but this is unlikely to cause anyone any harm. However, animosity is the product of other negative virtues such as jealousy and envy, or fear.

When working on feelings or actions of animosity, you need to first understand the underlying influence. With this, you can move forward.

apathy

Assist with developing an interest in, or feelings toward, a certain object or issue.

crystal sodalite

practice Apathy seems at odds with spiritual practice as a fundamental aspect of lightwork is natural curiosity and a desire to discover and learn. With apathy, you are unable to become enlightened, unable to progress and barriers are created to things that give you joy and pleasure.

Often the barrier is apathy itself although removing your lack of interest is one of the most difficult hurdles. In this case, you can look for alternatives, temporarily setting aside the issues to which you feel indifferent. There is nothing to be learned right now.

Exploring other things may assist to lessen the feeling of dispassion and help rekindle enthusiasm once felt or desired.

devotion

Assist in feeling connected to a person, object or cause, and to attract connection from the same.

crystal pink calcite

practice While you may confuse it with just love, devotion encompasses many virtues such as love, loyalty, fidelity, and honor. Devotion can also mean a commitment to a goal.

To affirm your devotion to anything, you can further your understanding of how that thing or object relates to you and how it impacts your life. In this understanding, you begin to realize its value – and it is this realization that helps you to maintain your positive connection. You can't be devoted to something that you do not value.

In crystal work, use devotion stones to focus on revealing true value while also investigating what barriers would break that value such that damaging situations or events can be avoided.

discipline

Assist with understanding or developing a set of rules or procedures and following them. Useful in training or in life practices.

crystal orange calcite, snowflake obsidian

practice While basic religions and laws provide some overarching life rules, your life can be made less chaotic if you also adopt a complementary personal set of guidelines that feel right for your own circumstances. You can become your own governor in terms of how you live in your personal space.

Rules can as simple as "I will meditate at the end of every day" or "I will not take drugs" – whatever works for you personally in a positive way.

With abiding by your own ruleset, you can define your boundaries without permanent constraint, as you can adapt and change them as you gain knowledge and experience. In this, you can reveal your life's purpose - and live it.

egotism

Help to abate or deflect the negative effects of selfishness, verbal self-reference or boasting. Promote humility and altruism.

crystal hematite

practice In some environments, self-promotion is a good virtue to master, especially in a competitive work situation. You don't want to undersell your abilities as though you're hiding under a rock! However, this must be balanced with some humility such that you don't become arrogant and unable to withstand criticism or rejection. Egotism can lead to isolation if left unchecked.

Exposure to the selfish behavior of others can also cause problems even when you are comfortable with your own level of humility. You can draw comparisons and erroneously use them as benchmarks in your own life. This can cause you to take actions and risks that are outside your norms.

In working to control your own egotism or to reduce the negative impact of others, you can focus on how your own actions affect others, and whether they positively affect your world. Some focus on the reflection element may help you to understand how others perceive you.

empathy

Help or develop identification with, or understanding of the experiences or feelings of another.

crystal rose quartz

practice In any lightwork, empathy is a vitally important part of your spirituality. It governs your ability not only to care for others but also your desire to provide help. Empathy is the true expression of selfless inward emotion toward another person or spirit.

In opening yourself to the feelings of others, and to see things from their perspective, you are in effect opening yourself to learning. It exposes you to messages and experiences that are not your own, thereby extending your possible sphere of knowledge. With this, you can co-mingle your own life experiences and interpret the meanings in a way that is mutually beneficial and positive.

Empathy is a keystone virtue for any lightworker and is particularly useful when used in conjunction with any of the elements in the psychic realm.

fear

Help to deal with the thoughts or emotions that cause discomfort, apprehension, dread or insecurity.

crystal black obsidian, rhodonite

practice Fear of any kind prevents you from moving forward. Some fear is well founded, being based on life experience which causes you to take alternative routes. However, when a fear creates a blockage or barrier, it will negatively impact your life as you become fixed and stuck.

In order to release fear blockages, you can focus on understanding the fear from either end, rather than the fear itself. What causes it and what will be the ramifications if you push through? In this way, you can imagine alternate possibilities and direct your focus rather to the outcomes and how you can affect them in a positive way. In this way, the fear itself becomes less important.

Include in grids when working on a specific problem or use to support another crystal if fear is an underlying problem or needs to be broken.

forgiveness

Help to ease feelings of resentment toward another.

crystal orange calcite

practice The affirmation "what's done is the past, what's possible is the future" is the keystone of forgiveness. Acceptance of the past is an integral part of changing your attitude to past wrongs. Forgiveness comes when you realize that your internal feelings of resentment are your own doing and that you are completely in control of how you move forward. You can forgive without forgetting.

While time to heal plays an important role, you can ease hurt by focusing on releasing yourself from being a victim of an event or action, and rather focusing on what you have learned. The mere fact that you survive beyond hurt tells you that forgiveness is possible, if not inevitable. You cannot un-spill milk, however, you can clean it up.

goodwill

Attract or give kindness or benevolence.

crystal magnesite, rose quartz

practice In lightwork, goodwill can be loosely interpreted as kindness – an action that usually makes you feel good regardless of whether you are giving or it or receiving it. There is always a way to show kindness, no matter how small, and often the only cost is self-sacrifice.

Developing goodwill needs to remove the focus on intent and outcome, both of which should only ever be that kindness affects something in a positive way. If kindness is given only to receive gratitude or to enhance reputation it is not goodwill – in this the intent is conditional and the outcome measurable, which is not ideal.

Goodwill comes when you show kindness that is unconditional and unmeasured, and that your capacity to give or receive kindness is unhindered in this respect. Often the best outcome is a simple thank you.

gratitude

Help to give or accept gratitude or thanks, receive recognition and achieve favorable outcomes.

crystal orange calcite

practice Feeling appreciated is an immensely joyful human emotion as it releases positive energy that you can then radiate into other parts of your life. It is up there with love, being kind of a score card on your daily activity. However, to be appreciated you must be able to also feel gratitude.

This gratitude is measurable. Are you looking for a simple kind word or acknowledgment of something done? Or do you want something greater such as recognition or fame? Maybe, you want to be rewarded in some material way. Often, if you don't receive the level of appreciation you expect, you can feel down or question your behavior – your gratitude will be shallow.

In all cases, gratitude provides positivity in both directions. As you understand what it is that you want in the form of appreciation, you can begin to understand what others feel when shown your own appreciation, and the positive impact it has. You can also learn to differentiate between real appreciation and just politeness.

When working on gratitude, incorporate reflection to further understanding.

humanity

Increase feelings toward human welfare and project humanitarian behavior.

crystal pink calcite

practice Humanitarianism extends goodwill into the physical world of action which comes in the form of help. In this effort, you remove all your prejudices and self-awareness, your actions becoming purely based on the common fact that you are human, surviving on a single planet. There is no distinction of gender, class, race, or species, and so on. You treat others equally and in a way that you would like to be treated yourself, on the most basic level.

Humanity taps into your most basic and primal instincts, leading you to behave in a way that is respectful of the current human conditions.

Like goodwill, humanitarianism should be unconditional.

humility

Assist with dispelling selfishness or ego. Attain modesty, grace, and humbleness. Be thankful without conditions.

crystal sodalite

practice Being self-confident is a wonderful expression, however, at times, you may need to temper this with humility so that you are not drawn into conceit when communicating with others.

Humility allows you to acknowledge that you simply can't know everything and that there is always still much to be learned. It opens light channels to new ideas and experiences.

When working on humility, use crystals that also encompass empathy, goodwill, and humanity.

See also egotism.

judgment

Aid your ability to make good judgments or to be judged favorably. Useful when dealing with issues of discrimination.

crystal cordierite, snowflake obsidian

practice Good judgment is not just about making choices or agreeing with others on what is good and bad. Your ability to discern what is right and wrong is a very personal virtue – a judgment must be right or wrong for you irrespective of the views of others. In this, you must be careful not to judge others simply because you disagree.

To be judged favorably by others you need to be firm in your beliefs while remaining open to learning. You must also be in complete acceptance that not everyone will judge you favorably at all times. You are all always imperfect.

Focus on discernment should lead you to look inward, to find appreciation in yourself - and to like what you see.

nurture

Assist in any area that is concerned with the protection of something that is new or cherished, and where development is encouraged or desired.

crystal pink calcite, red jasper

practice The things you hold dear to you, which give you joy and make you feel good, need to be protected so they continue to have a positive impact on your life. If you fail to identify those things and fail to treat them with care, you risk diminishing their positivity or losing them completely. Once lost, it is difficult to regain them.

Nurture is first about being aware of the things you cherish. What do you have that you could not possibly be without? What could not possibly be replaced? It may be something like your family bonds, or your spirituality. It rarely includes material things or activities you undertake.

Once you have identified the true elements, you can begin to care for them in a nurturing way, protecting them from any form of negative influence and allowing them to grow.

peace

Help to restore calm or harmony, achieve a state where thoughts are restful and recuperative. Help to subdue negative influences.

crystal howlite, rhodonite, shungite

practice When stress disrupts your peace you subject yourself to more than just mind chaos. It permeates into the physical world and leads you to all sorts of illnesses which mean you are then dealing with two issues, one mental and one physical.

Finding peace is key to solving many of life's issues as it enables you to focus your thoughts on positivity. This does not mean you need to spend all day meditating! You can be very active, yet still at peace.

When working with crystals, focus on each of the elements that bring stress into your life and work to resolving each one individually. In this way, problems become small pieces easily addressed instead of one big chaotic and seemingly insurmountable mass. As each problem is resolved, and you enjoy the process of just "doing", you are lead to a more holistic and peaceful state.

perfection

Help to achieve perfection or goals. Can also be used to attune with nature where perfection is innate and unable to be contrived.

crystal lepidolite, tiger's eye

practice Without imagination, it is difficult to perceive anything that exists being improved in some way. This creates a blockage to new ideas, new paths and new perception as it keeps you stuck in a world of just reality where you accept that everything is all that it can ever be.

In lightwork, however, you generally believe that nothing is perfect unless found in nature, created by some sort of God or unaltered by human influence. You are therefore naturally idealistic, believing that many things can be changed for the better.

In working with ideals, you are really defining your values and pursuing the perfection of those values for use in everyday life. It helps you to set goals and move forward in a positive way.

prejudice

Help to dispel judgmental feelings toward things that are unfamiliar or where knowledge is limited. Help to change or build attitudes.

crystal jadeite, rhodonite

practice Your experiences add to your personal book of knowledge which you can then tap into to form opinions and attitudes. Sometimes you may be influenced by the experience of others too. However, in lightwork you know that knowledge is never complete and that there is always still more to learn. When you open yourself to learning and further experiences, you acknowledge that your attitudes are able to change, even though you may at times be uncomfortable with things that are unfamiliar.

With an expectation that your attitudes will probably change over time, you can dispel prejudice as just a temporary idea. While it is healthy to hold opinions and have views, these can only ever relate to just the here and now. They may not be solid reasons to move you forward in a particular way.

Your ability to change and adapt as you gather life experience is a most precious virtue.

respect

Help to hold, or be held with respect and treat or be treated with kindness.

crystal magnesite, serpentine

practice Respect is often interpreted as just admiration, in observance of some achievement or ability. However, respect has far more wide-reaching qualities and, in crystal work, governs how you relate to others on a daily basis. A lack of respect will lead to all sorts of negativity.

How and why you hold respect for anything should be based purely on kindness. Are you able to be kind to something that has not achieved much? Is kindness only ever given when deserved or earned? Or is respect only ever warranted when it is measurable by some form of activity?

To respect is to be kind, no matter what the circumstance dictates. While you may not always understand others or even the purpose of a static object, to be respectful accepts that it exists in its own right and is traveling on its own path over which you have no right of control.

safety

Assist with feelings of being free from danger and undesirable outcomes. Also useful when working with protection elements.

crystal rhodochrosite

practice Closely related to fear, your desire for actions to not cause any harm can be relevant in any of the spiritual realms.

While fear prevents you from moving forward for fear of harm, safety focuses on the outcomes when you do move forward. It is particularly apparent when there is some perceived degree of risk or uncertainty that would work to your detriment.

While you work to overcome or understand fear in order to move forward, you can also focus on what represents safety along the way, and in the final arrival of the outcome. If the abolition of fear makes you blast into the unknown, you can be mindful of safety measures that you can implement to help ease your path. These measures can provide a kind of checklist or series of gates – checkpoints in life's journey if you like. Developing a firm idea of what constitutes safety will assist you when encountering unforeseen dangers and hurdles.

truth

Strengthen feelings of belief, seek honesty and speak honestly.

crystal apatite, pyrite

practice The truth element covers a range of sub-elements such as honesty, authenticity, deception, suspicion, sincerity and integrity, and so on. The pursuit of truth can be both positive and negative. However, if you can't believe something to be factual or real, there is concern over truth.

In seeking the truth, you are really seeking to either affirm what you already believe or to reveal something that is concealed. In affirmations, you open your existing beliefs to challenge. Can more information change what you already believe to be truthful? In revelation, can you get new information upon which you can form new beliefs?

In either case, you must maintain an open mind. You must also be mindful that you cannot exist peacefully if you constantly question your beliefs to the point where you believe nothing. Truth comes when you relate it to how you exist today.

will

Strengthen personal determination.

crystal hypersthene

practice As you journey, there will be obstacles you must navigate and hazards you can only try to avoid. These are the whirlpools in the river of life. Sometimes even swimming against the river's current seems too hard a task and it is easier to just go with the flow.

However, the flow may not always take you in the right direction. To overcome obstacles and continue on, you must adopt some personal will to do so. You cannot just resort to external help – relying on someone else to fix it. This can be difficult as there is always plenty of help on offer.

In crystal work, you strengthen your will by focusing on the goal, imagining the positive outcome and visualizing yourself in that positive situation. This may encompass working with many elements as all go to support your personal determination.

wisdom realm

akashic record

Access thoughts and knowledge that exist in the astral plane.

crystal labradorite

practice All knowledge and all life experience of every living thing are said to exist in a complete book of records in the astral, or etheric plane. It is commonly referred to as the Akashic record.

To access this knowledge and apply its messages to your everyday life, you must first focus on your ability to connect with the higher realms and also your complete acceptance of any messages received – without prejudice and with gratitude. Messages are then open to your personal interpretation and application. Therefore this element should be used in conjunction with other elements relating to wisdom and messages.

Be mindful that not all information is communicated in a way which is readily understood. This element serves to provide you with possibilities based on the experience of others.

clarity

Seek clear and distinct understanding that is free from ambiguity.

crystal black obsidian, orange calcite

practice When working on problems or specific issues, the outcomes will always be determined by your ability to understand your thoughts. At times you may feel there is no clear way forward. Many choices appear and this causes you to hesitate.

When you hesitate, you often put this down to life being a jumbled mess of uncertainties, and indeed this is true. However, when you fear to make the wrong choices, you miss the point that life itself is the real joyous outcome.

In working with clarity, it is vital to understand that however you proceed, the path chosen is the right one for you at that moment. What is clear is that there is something you must learn here, even if the outcome is not as expected. Practice and enjoyment of the path will eventually lead you to full understanding.

communication

Improve the exchange of thoughts and ideas, both spoken and transmitted.

crystal goldstone

practice Communication can be internal (yourself), external (other people) or with energies in the higher realms. Opening light channels facilitates this communication in a way that is both supportive and productive.

However you choose to communicate, it is right for you at this moment. It does not mean that you must gabble on, you can even choose to sit in silence, lost in your own thoughts or intently consumed by the thoughts of others.

Each communication is valuable as it adds to your own body of wisdom.

comprehension

Improve ability to understand or perceive unfamiliar ideas. Improve knowledge.

crystal labradorite, optical calcite

practice There are things you can learn just by habitual repetition and some things you do not necessarily need to understand – it just is. However, when you need to understand things that are new, unfamiliar and foreign, you can sometimes be blocked by your current level of knowledge and natural biases.

Clearing paths to new ideas and finding new directions is about removing those blockages or at least setting them aside.

In this way you become open to new understanding, acknowledging that life is about constant learning.

concentration

Assist in focusing on a particular path, idea or issue.

crystal optical calcite

practice At times your thoughts can seem like a jumbled mess while at other times you may feel that you are drained, unable to concentrate on a single activity. This is especially true as your life gets busier and you become more controlled by external matters.

When you need to calm your mind and focus on a single issue that needs either resolution, renewal or strengthening, you can intensify the thought process by focusing on areas that give you the most concern.

For influences that have a positive impact on your life, such as love, and prosperity you can also enhance their prominence through thought amplification.

decisions

Assist in finding a conclusion, determination or settlement where one or more choices are available.

crystal cordierite, malachite, pyrite

practice Having choices is a great thing however at some point you need to make decisions about which of those choices you pursue. When trying to make decisions that ultimately will bring something to a conclusion, you can be stuck when you are presented with choices that you see only as final.

When this prevents you moving forward you need to view your choice in a different light. Instead of seeing the finality – the "no going back" option - you can focus on the positives beyond the conclusion. Any decision will present new opportunities and views, and further choices.

insight

Assist in understanding the true nature of things or the underlying truth. Help to shed light on issues.

crystal labradorite, sardonyx

practice In all things there are underlying truths - call it the basis of being. At times this can become clouded especially in a busy life full of activity.

Gaining insight relates to removing the clouds and looking at the object or subject as a singular thing, being separate from everything else.

What is at its core? What is its basis for being? Once you have looked at the object in isolation you can then begin to understand how it relates to everything else, how it plays a part and how you can use it to fulfill your life.

In crystal work, focus on the core issue first to gain insight into everything surrounding it.

intellect

Ask or be asked pertinent questions and give or receive relevant and clear answers.

crystal amethyst

practice Simple communication does not always need to stimulate your intellect, however, such communication always brings forth creativity and adds to your wisdom. It also allows your mind energy to flow which fosters curiosity and new beginnings.

In focusing on intellectual stimulation, you can be empowered to act and try new things, which will, in turn, assist your spiritual growth.

mental clarity

Reduce stress and increase focus. Decrease the number of issues to be dealt with or processed in a single time.

crystal scolecite

practice Concentrating on a single issue will generally result in that issue being either resolved or its effect diminished. When you try to juggle multiple issues or you fail to see things through, you decrease your ability to cope with multiple threads.

Dealing with issues in a logical, prioritized order will prevent your problems from spiraling out of control causing stress and mental fatigue.

When working with crystals, allocate a stone to each problem and deal with each separately.

regeneration

Allow new thoughts and ideas to change perception. Discard outdated or obsolete beliefs.

crystal girasol

practice Letting go of old influences and beliefs can transform your life by facilitating the adoption of new ideas and practices.

In crystal work, regeneration symbolizes not only new beginnings but also changing attitudes to past activities or experiences.

For instance, a bad habit or bad experience can be retained as a barrier to spiritual growth as you fail to move on. The habit becomes your "norm" despite its negative implications. The experience becomes your life pivot point as you categorize everything as either happening before or after the experience, even if the experience itself has no relevance.

In working on regeneration you are opening yourself to new things that will impact your life in a positive way, allowing you to grow and move forward.

resolution

Determine a final path or intention, form an opinion or find a settlement.

crystal malachite, pyrite, snowflake obsidian

practice If something troubles you, it will continue to cause discomfort until a resolution is found. Discomfort, worry, or anxiety come from things that are not understood, have not worked out the way you planned, or have changed course from the original path. When you seek to bring an end to things, you must first find a resolution. This is the only way you can see beyond the discomfort and move forward. While the final outcome may not be the actual end of the thing that creates the discomfort, simply understanding the problem may be a resolution in itself. An "end" may not come in the cessation of the external influence.

It is human nature to concentrate on a disruptive issue by focusing on the thing that creates the disruption – hoping that it will stop, hoping that it will somehow change. This is very externally focused. In practice, it is better to focus on how it makes you feel – this is the only element over which you have absolute control. The question then becomes, what can I do to feel differently? It is only then that resolution is possible and choices can be formed.

kyanite rough

agate

The clearing nature of the agate stone makes it useful in any element that is benefited by clear paths and open channels. In clearing the way, agate allows energy to flow freely. It is often used in sliced form as a standing geode or disc but is also useful in tumble stone form. Use agate in a beacon to allow energy to radiate. Select colors can be used to cleanse auras and chakras.

colors and care

Agate comes in a wide variety of colors from iridescent blues to vibrant pinks and deep browns and is noted for its layered and multi-colored banding. Agate is resistant to scratches and may be immersed. Care should be taken with sun and heat exposure so that colors do not fade.

amazonite

Amazonite brings strength to elements that require intense focus. Use in a grid when dealing with issues that require strong actions. Also, use to abate feelings of panic or when the energy flow needs to be directed quickly.

colors and care

Usually pale to vivid green, or pale sky blue, and it is often dyed which will be apparent if the color appears too uniform. Amazonite is a soft stone and will break easily. Do not expose to sunlight and do not immerse or heat.

amethyst

Amethyst is one of the most diverse crystals covering a wide spectrum of elements. It's a favorite in jewelry of all kinds and commonly appears in geode or cluster form.

Use amethyst to work on any of its core elements and always keep it in your collection as it will enhance the frequency of any other crystal, particularly quartz-based crystals.

colors and care

Amethyst comes in purple, violet, lilac or pale pink. Deepest purples attract the highest values. It is fairly resilient to both scratches and immersion, although heat and sunlight may affect its color.

ametrine

Ametrine is a mixture of amethyst and citrine. Use ametrine when working on relationships as a base stone or in support of another stone. As it easily faceted, it is attractive in jewelry.

colors and care

Ametrine can be translucent plain purple and may often show areas of smoke or yellow. The most prized stones graduate from orange to purple. Ametrine is often referred to as bolivianite or trystine. It is fairly resilient to both scratches and immersion, although heat and sunlight may affect its color.

apatite

aquamarine

Use opaque green or blue apatite as a focus stone in a grid or combine transparent apatite with other stones intended to open channels or provide paths. It is useful to support any stone involved with resolving blockages. Any type of apatite should always be used when asking for a truth to be revealed or where dishonesty may be an issue.

colors and care

Apatite is usually green-yellow, blue, lilac, purple or violet. It will scratch and shatter easily and should not be immersed, although it will withstand sunlight and heat. Due to its brittleness, it is not recommended for jewelry. Beware of imitation transparent apatite which is often colored glass.

Aquamarine is a stone of clear connections. Use it when working on any of the psychic realm elements. It is attractive in jewelry and can be used either polished or rough.

colors and care

Aquamarine is usually found in pale green to pale blue although many pure blues have been treated to remove the green hue. It is resistant to scratches and may be immersed.

aventurine

Aventurine is a great crystal to use for anything to do with the material world and for finding stability and balance. Pair with citrine when working on wealth in grids and beacons.

colors and care

Aventurine is opaque light to dark green. It can be banded and often has gray/white patches. As a member of the quartz group, it is resistant to scratching and may be immersed as well as exposed to sunlight and heat.

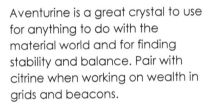

black obsidian

Black obsidian is useful when working with elements that seek to increase transparency or to see through issues. Always use in any grid designed for the psychic realm. It is not recommended for jewelry.

colors and care

Black obsidian in not strictly a crystal, rather it is volcanic glass and is commonly black to dark deep brown with a silver glass like sheen. Many colored obsidians such as blue and pink are modern and manufactured colored glass sold as colored obsidian. Obsidian is quite hard, may be immersed and exposed to sunlight or heat. Replace broken crystals as obsidian dust may be harmful.

black onyx

Black onyx is useful to calm and heal. Use it to seek guidance from spirit guides and when working on spirituality or beliefs in general. Polished stones are good when worn as jewelry.

colors and care

Black onyx is usually black with white/silver patches or ribbons. For the red and yellow varieties see sardonyx. Black onyx is very hard and resistant to scratches. It can be immersed and exposed to sunlight or heat.

blue fluorite

Blue fluorite deals with anything related to energy flow and is most useful in the emotional realm, however, it can also be used in the energy realm. Use blue fluorite in a grid as a base stone or to support any other stone.

colors and care

Known for its vivid translucent deep blue, blue fluorite may have aspects of pink and yellow. It is a brittle stone that is easily scratched, so handle with care. Due to its brittleness, it is not recommended for use in jewelry. It may be immersed as well as exposed to sunlight.

blue quartz

bronzite

Use blue quartz for any element in the emotional realm. Polished tumble stones are useful when worn as jewelry.

colors and care

Blue quartz is usually pale to deep blue due to the inclusion of the mineral dumortierite which gives natural clear quartz a bluish color. It is hard and resistant to scratches and can be immersed, as well as exposed to sunlight and heat.

Bronzite represents strength and can be used to support any issues that require concerted effort for a length of time. It is also useful to provide support in times of weakness, either in mind, body or spirit.

colors and care

Look for bronzite stones that show an even distribution of the copper color against the darker brown background. Bronzite is very durable although some scratching may occur. It can be immersed.

carnelian

chalcedony

Carnelian is a powerful crystal to use when working with conflict issues and dealing with anything to do with the past. When used as a support stone in a grid, it will amplify the element and provide a quicker solution. Carnelian is best used in grids.

colors and care

Carnelian is a variety of chalcedony. It is usually orange to a deep brownish red and is opaque with a lustrous sheen when polished. In rough form, it is an orange/brown version of regular gray chalcedony and should be treated the same.

Chalcedony is the stone of the mind and can be used in any element that is thought based. It is particularly useful in connecting with the higher realms, and can be used as a focus stone in a grid or to support any of the higher realm crystals.

colors and care

The name chalcedony covers a variety of crystals including agate and is therefore often confused with other stones. For crystal work, choose an opaque grey-white, opaque pale blue or lilac stone. For green stones, see chrysoprase. Avoid stones with deeply intense colors that may have been dyed. It is fairly resilient to scratches, can be immersed and exposed to sunlight or heat.

chrysoprase

cinnabarite

Chrysoprase is used to attract or protect a certain state, particularly prosperity. For grids, poles, and beacons, it is best used in its rough, unpolished state. Polished tumble stones are appropriate for jewelry and smaller pieces can be carried as keepsakes to attract good financial outcomes.

Cinnabarite is known as the merchant's stone and can be used to attract wealth or to facilitate good outcomes in business dealings. Use it in grids or to support any element in the material realm. It is not recommended for jewelry and care should be taken with broken crystals.

colors and care

Chrysoprase is pale green on white. As it is a variety of chalcedony, it is fairly resilient to scratches, can be immersed and exposed to sunlight or heat.

colors and care

Cinnabarite is opaque white with red to burgundy flecks or patches. As it contains traces of mercury, it may be harmful if broken down. It is best used in polished tumble stone form. It will scratch and shatter easily. Do not expose to heat or sunlight and do not immerse in water.

citrine

Citrine is generally accepted as the stone of luck and good fortune so use it when dealing with anything in the material realm. It is good when worn as jewelry and smaller stones can be carried as keepsakes. Place citrine in a beacon to attract abundance.

colors and care

Citrine is typically yellow to orange in color however it is quite rare in its natural form. Most citrine is heat treated amethyst which turns from purple to yellow – this is an acceptable substitute in crystal work. It is fairly resilient to both scratches and immersion, although heat and sunlight may affect its color especially if it is amethyst based.

clear quartz

Quartz of any kind is a powerful amplifier and energy stimulant. Use clear quartz to support any crystal in a grid where a specific quality is not required. Include clear quartz in a beacon to enhance the surrounding crystals.

colors and care

Clear quartz is perhaps the most common of all the crystals. It is usually clear and colorless, often showing some inclusions which may enhance their value such as phantom clear quartz. It may be immersed, exposed to sunlight and heat however it will break and chip easily.

clinochlore

cobalt aura

Clinochlore is useful in all aspects of the higher realms, especially when calling spirit guides and angels.

Cobalt aura can be used to assist recovery from illness and also to strengthen ties. It is commonly used when working on any of the psychic elements and can be useful as a focus stone in grids.

colors and care

Clinochlore is sold under a variety of names, the most common being seraphinite. It is easily recognized having a deep green base with white inclusions resembling feathers. Being a chlorite, clinochlore is very soft and easily scratched. When held it will feel almost oily and will produce a green powder when damaged. Do not expose clinochlore to heat and do not immerse in water. Replace damaged stones.

colors and care

Cobalt aura is a treated variety of quartz so should be handled as quartz. It may be immersed, exposed to sunlight and heat however it will break and chip easily.

cordierite

Cordierite represents choices and will assist in decision making. Use it in a grid when asking specific questions where directions are needed. Cordierite can also indicate travel or a change in direction.

colors and care

Cordierite comes in an opaque form or in a translucent form which is known as iolite. In either case, both cordierite and iolite are interchangeable. Look for deep blues in cordierite and strong violet in iolite. Both will shatter easily. Do not immerse or expose to sunlight or heat.

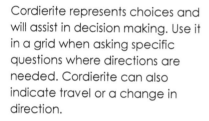

dumortierite

Dumortierite is the stone of travel and will indicate a journey to be undertaken. Combine with elements that relate to places and buildings, in particular places of work and study.

colors and care

Look for dumortierite opaque dark blue, however lighter blues are also acceptable. It is often confused with blue quartz or blue lace agate. Dumortierite is fairly resilient to scratches and may be immersed, exposed to sunlight and heat.

epidote

fuchsite

Epidote literally means addition so can be used in with any element that seeks to add or attract.

colors and care

Look for stones that are olive green in color which may be translucent to opaque. Epidote can be immersed, exposed to sunlight and heat, however it will break and chip easily.

Fuchsite is closely related to aventurine (which contains fuchsite) in that it provides stability, however, it is also protective. It can be used in with any elements as a stone of protection from negative influence. It is good for use in grids and worn as jewelry.

colors and care

Look for fuchsite stones that are opaque and consistently pale green in color with some flecks of darker green. It is often found with red flecks (ruby fuchsite) which strengthens the stone's meaning.

Fuchsite is a member of the quartz group and therefore is fairly resilient to scratches and may be immersed, exposed to sunlight and heat.

garnet

Garnet is a good crystal to use when dealing with health related issues or issues in the physical realm. Use it in a grid as a grounding stone to support anything that relates to growth or renewal.

colors and care

Garnet comes in a variety of colors from almost black to deep reds, blues, and greens, often with flecks of lighter colors. Look for darker stones for crystal use. It is resistant to scratches and may be immersed, exposed to sunlight and heat.

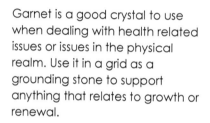

girasol

Girasol represents new things, renewal, and rebirth in both the physical and spiritual worlds. Girasol can also indicate maternal influences. It is good when worn as jewelry.

colors and care

Girasol is a form of white opal and often shows some opalescence. It is often manufactured from glass which is a reasonable substitute when natural girasol is unavailable. Look for stones that are milky white in appearance. It is brittle and easily scratched although it can be immersed and exposed to sunlight and heat.

goldstone

Goldstone assists with learning and communication of any kind, either in the physical or spiritual world.

colors and care

Goldstone is not a natural crystal and it is usually a form of manufactured glass, however, it is used in crystal work because of the pigments and inclusions used in its making, and glass which itself is made from natural sand. Goldstone is often found in either deep royal blue or green. Like glass, it is brittle and is not resistant to scratching or chipping. It can be immersed and exposed to sunlight or heat.

green fluorite

Green fluorite deals with anything related to energy balance. Use it in a grid as a base stone or to support any other stone. Green fluorite is particularly useful in the energy realm. Due to its brittleness, it is not recommended for use in jewelry.

colors and care

Look for green fluorite in light to dark green. It is reasonably brittle so handle with care. Do not immerse or expose it to sunlight or heat.

hematite

howlite

Hematite is best used as a grounding crystal and to support any stone in a grid except higher and psychic realm elements. Be careful when pairing with crystals designed to project and attract as hematite will negate their influence. Always use it when dealing with elements in the protective realm. It is good worn as jewelry.

Howlite is useful for all elements requiring peace and calm. It is a highly restorative crystal when used in a grid or worn as jewelry. Always use howlite in the meditative realm.

colors and care

Howlite is available is many colors including blue and green however natural howlite is usually white with a gray spider web pattern. As it is very porous, natural howlite is often dyed blue to resemble turquoise (sold as turquenite), or green to resemble chrysocolla. It is quite brittle and will scratch. Howlite should not be immersed.

colors and care

Look for hematite that is deep red to gray/black and pure black. It is known for its shine when polished. Make sure you purchase natural hematite (not magnetic) and not artificially produced hematine (magnetic) where possible. Hematite is somewhat brittle and will scratch easily. It can be immersed, however, may lose its luster if exposed to heat.

hypersthene

Hypersthene represents power and can be used to strengthen any element. Use it in a grid to support other stones, or carry a small crystal when physical exertion is required.

colors and care

Hypersthene is related to bronzite however it usually appears in dark brown to black or green. Look for stones that show pearly white bands or streaking. Hypersthene is very durable although some scratching may occur. It can be immersed, exposed to heat or sunlight.

jadeite

Use jadeite when working with any clearing element, breaking free of something or removing influences. It is best used in polished form and is also very good in jewelry.

colors and care

Jadeite is usually opaque green but may also be found in pink. It is often called buddstone. It is brittle and will shatter easily. Do not immerse or expose to heat.

kunzite

Kunzite is a universal stone that is useful in many situations. It governs communication, revelation, light and happiness. Use as a base stone in a grid and as a support stone for any element. It is good when worn as jewelry (polished) and as part of a beacon (rough) but keep it out of direct sunlight.

colors and care

Kunzite is a pink variety of spudomene. Treated kunzite is vivid green (often marketed as hiddenite which is quite rare), however, it will fade back to pink if heated. It is brittle and will shatter easily. Do not expose kunzite to sunlight as even the pink will fade and do not immerse it.

kyanite

Use kyanite when working with any healing element. As it is quite brittle, use it in rough form in beacons and in polished form for grids and jewelry. As it is often found as polished flat stones, it is ideal as a keepsake.

colors and care

Kyanite is usually a soft blue with silvery veins but can be found in deep blue translucent varieties. Kyanite should be handled with care as it is brittle and will shatter very easily especially in its rough state. Do not immerse or expose it to heat.

labradorite

Labradorite is useful for any element in the wisdom realm or when information from the higher realm is sought. It indicates messages that are to be received or given.

colors and care

Labradorite is usually dark gray to greenish with some degree of translucency although it is often seen with the iridescent colors of blue, yellow, and green resembling an oily luster known as labradorescence. It is sometimes sold under the name spectrolite. It is hard and resistant to scratches and can be immersed as well as exposed to sunlight and heat.

lapis lazuli

Lapis lazuli is prized for its vivid blue color and its use can be widely seen in antiquities. In crystal work, it represents both the past and the higher realms. Use it in a grid or wear as jewelry.

colors and care

Lapis lazuli is usually found in deep blue, often with golden flecks and veins. It is not actually a crystal, rather it is a rock so therefore quite hard and resistant to scratching. It may be immersed.

lepidolite

magnesite

Lepidolite has varied uses in crystal work as a good grounding stone when trying to achieve change. It can be used as a base stone for any of the elements or as a support stone in a grid. Lepidolite can be worn as jewelry and often small pieces (polished) can be kept in a pocket or purse as a keepsake.

Use magnesite as an attraction stone and pair with any element that is intended to provide a positive influence or outcome. Magnesite will also assist with anything in the virtuous realm.

colors and care

Look for lepidolite stones that are pale to deep pink or lilac with silvery white patching. Lepidolite is quite soft and will shatter easily. Do not immerse or expose to sunlight.

colors and care

Magnesite stones can be clear or white. Look for stones that include some weak yellows. If the crystal is broken, dispose of it thoughtfully as it can be harmful if ingested. Can be exposed to sunlight but should not be immersed.

malachite

Malachite is a powerful crystal of change. Use it in any grid that seeks to reverse a situation or to promote change in the opposite direction. It is not recommended for jewelry.

colors and care

Malachite is generally a vivid green in variable shades of light to dark. It often includes spots of blue, which is its close cousin azurite. Do not expose to heat and do not immerse it in water. Malachite will scratch and shatter easily and may be harmful if ground to a dust. Some synthetically produced malachite will appear unnatural in color and banding.

mookaite

Mookaite is a strong influencer of male energies. Use it in a grid or as jewelry to attract or strengthen male bonds, to develop masculine traits or fatherly instincts. It is useful in issues relating to paternity, family, bonds or fertility. Combine mookaite with red jasper to balance male/female energy.

colors and care

Mookaite is a variety of jasper found predominantly in Australia and is often called Australian jasper. Varieties found in other countries are generally known as radiolarite. Both are usually variegated red/brown/yellow with stripes and patches. Mookaite is resistant to scratching and can be immersed.

moss agate

nuummite

Use moss agate when working with earthy problems or to help connect with energies that transcend through the body to the heavenly realms. It is useful in grids as a soul stone or to support other stones such as grounding stones.

colors and care

Moss agate is typically deep green on a milky white background. Unlike normal agate, moss agate is not banded. It is fairly resilient to both scratches, sunlight, heat and immersion.

Nuummite is useful for any element which requires mind travel such as daydreaming, meditation or astral travel. It taps into the subconscious plane and helps to connect with the higher realms.

colors and care

Look for stark black stones that show white or gold inclusions or banding below the surface. Natural nuummite is quite rare and may substituted with snowflake obsidian or black onyx. It is reasonably hard but may scratch. Due to its rarity, natural nuummite should be handled with some care. It can be immersed.

optical calcite

orange calcite

Optical calcite can be used when working with higher realm elements or for finding options to complex problems. It assists with making decisions on forward paths. Carry a small piece as a keepsake when the mind is busy or dealing with multiple threads.

Add orange calcite to grids when working on mental issues such as clarity and focus. Wear it as jewelry or carry as a keepsake for all elements in the psychic realm.

colors and care

Optical calcite is sometimes known as iceland calcite or iceland spar. It is usually colorless with the appearance and shape of an ice cube or in smooth shapes when tumbled. It is fairly resistant to heavy scratching and may be immersed.

colors and care

Look for orange calcite stones that are golden orange with some pale cream flecks. It can be used in rough or polished form. Orange calcite is resistant to heavy scratching and may be immersed.

orange selenite

Orange selenite is commonly called moonstone and it governs any element that is periodic in nature, such as biorhythmic balance. Use it when balancing energy flows. Orange selenite is good when worn as jewelry.

colors and care

Selenite is a variety of gypsum and can be quite soft, therefore it can be scratched and chipped easily. Do not immerse or expose to sunlight.

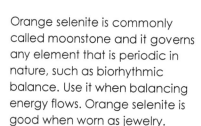

peridot

Peridot is a good conductor of light and can be used in any element that seeks to increase energy. It is also the stone of happiness and can be included in grids, beacons, and poles or worn as jewelry.

colors and care

Look for small epidote stones in pale to deep green. It is sometimes sold as a less expensive alternative to emerald. It is very hard and is resistant to scratching and may be immersed.

pietersite

Pietersite is a combination of tiger's eye and jasper so it helps to balance male/female energy. As a stone of the past, its presence will help communication with older beings.

colors and care

Pietersite is usually deep brown to burnt orange in color and often has ribbons of gold or blue. The ribbons can be either distinct or mossy in appearance. It is resistant to scratching and can be immersed.

pink calcite

Similar to rose quartz, pink calcite is useful when working with difficult relationships or friendships that have been broken. It can help any element in the virtuous realm that deals with external influences, or help to foster internal elements.

colors and care

Look for pink calcite stones that are consistent in color with a milky white patched appearance. Some imperfections are desirable. It is often called mangano calcite. Calcite is resistant to scratching and may be immersed and exposed to sunlight.

purple fluorite

pyrite

Purple fluorite deals with anything related to energy amplification. Use it in a grid as a base stone or to support any other stone. Purple fluorite is particularly useful in the higher and energy realms. Due to its brittleness, it is not recommended for use in jewelry.

colors and care

Purple fluorite is often confused with amethyst. Look for stones that are deep purple to lilac with some banding. It is brittle and easily scratched so handle with care.

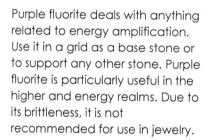

Commonly referred to as fool's gold, pyrite is a powerful generator of change. It is best used in rough, unpolished form and it can be used with almost any element to increase its influence. Like its mineral composition, pyrite is considered unstable and in nature is constantly being reformed.

Pyrite is also useful when seeking answers or truth and resolving deception. It is best used in grids.

colors and care

Look for pyrite stones that are evenly formed and contain no other visible minerals. Because of its high iron content, pyrite should not be immersed as it will begin to decompose. It is resistant to scratching and may be exposed to sunlight.

red jasper

rhodochrosite

Red jasper is a strong influencer of feminine energies. Use it in a grid or as jewelry to attract or strengthen female bonds, to develop feminine traits or to nurture motherly instincts. It is useful on any issues relating to pregnancy or fertility. Use with mookaite to balance male/female energy.

colors and care

Red jasper is a variety of chalcedony and a close cousin of carnelian. It is usually opaque red to brown in color, often with prominent cream to dark brown spots and webs. It is resistant to scratching and can be immersed.

Rhodochrosite is a protective crystal and useful when dealing with anything in the protective realm. Place in a beacon to protect from negative influences.

colors and care

Look for rhodochrosite stones that are pink/orange to vibrant red. Rhodochrosite is comparatively soft and will break easily. Colors may fade in long exposure to sunlight however it can be immersed.

rhodonite

Use rhodonite in any grid that seeks to repel or reverse an external negative influence. It is particularly useful in the virtuous realm and good when worn as jewelry.

colors and care

Rhodonite is usually soft pink when opaque and red when transparent, both with gray/black patches. These colors may fade in long exposure to sunlight. It can be immersed.

rose quartz

Rose quartz is one of the most recognized crystals and is commonly used to attract or deepen feelings of love. Include it in a beacon or use it as a focus stone in a grid for any element involving love, romance, relationships, and self-perception. Polished stones are good when worn as jewelry.

colors and care

Rose quartz is commonly opaque pale to deep pink and can also be translucent. Never immerse, expose to sunlight or heat as the color may fade.

sardonyx

Sardonyx helps to build awareness and understanding. Use in a grid as a support stone or wear as jewelry.

colors and care

Sardonyx is a red variety of onyx from the agate family of crystals and is usually brown to deep red with bands of white or brown/black. It is hard and resistant to scratches. It can be immersed and exposed to sunlight.

scolecite

Scolecite is known for its ability to help "see through" complex problems and to filter out noise. Use scolecite for grounding when dealing with issues that have many aspects.

colors and care

Scolecite in its natural state is needle-like in appearance and usually only valued by collectors. Look for polished tumble stones for use in crystal work. It is not recommended for jewelry and should not be immersed.

serpentine

Use serpentine in a grid when dealing with negative issues. Always pair with an energy stone.

colors and care

Serpentine is found in opaque green with banding or white to pale green patches. As serpentine contains trace amounts of asbestos, only use it in polished form and handle with care. Dispose of broken crystals thoughtfully. It is not recommended for jewelry and should not be heated or immersed.

shungite

Shungite is a calming stone and can be used to subdue influences or repel negativity. Shungite also represents purity and will provide protection and safety in grids or when worn as jewelry.

colors and care

Look for deeply colored stones. Some white veining is acceptable. Shungite is hard and resistant to scratches. It can be immersed and exposed to sunlight.

smoky quartz

Smoky quartz is a powerful amplifier and energy stimulant. It is useful as a support stone in any kind of grid and should always be included when dealing with clearing issues.

colors and care

Smoky quartz is clear to dark brown or black to gray, transparent to translucent. Never immerse smoky quartz, expose it to sunlight or heat as the color will fade.

snowflake obsidian

Use snowflake obsidian in the same way as black obsidian in any virtuous realm element, particularly where a speedier or amplified solution or resolution to a negative situation is needed.

colors and care

Sometimes called apache tears or pele's tears, snowflake obsidian contains cristobalite which gives it the white snowflakes. Treat in the same manner as black obsidian. It is not recommended for jewelry.

sodalite

sunstone

Sodalite will help with energy flows and clearing blockages, cleaning negative emotions on the way through. Carry it when smudging or use it in a grid.

colors and care

Look for sodalite stones that are dark blue with white veining and a dull luster. Varieties include hackmanite, which starts off white then turns pink if exposed to sunlight, and lazurite which is usually a deeper blue to purple. It is easily cracked and scratched. Do not immerse.

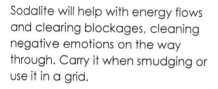

Sunstone radiates energy from within and therefore is useful in any lightbody work or aura strengthening. Use it in grids to support other stones or wear it as jewelry. It may also be placed in beacons to help radiate the light of other crystals.

colors and care

Look for pink to orange opaque sunstone varieties that become translucent on the outer surface rather than wholly transparent. Sunstone is hard and resistant to scratches. It can be immersed and exposed to heat.

tiger's eye

turquoise

Tiger's eye represents strong male influences. When used in a grid, tiger's eye will assist grounding and finding a connection with the natural world.

One of the most highly prized of the ancient crystals, turquoise has many uses, particularly in all matters relating to health. Use it in a grid as either a soul stone or a support stone. Old civilizations used turquoise as an indication of health believing it changed color according to the health of the individual wearing it as jewelry.

colors and care

Tiger's eye is a member of the quartz group and is sometimes called falcon eye when predominantly blue in color. It is hard and resistant to scratches. It can be immersed and exposed to heat.

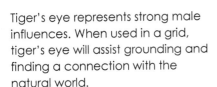

colors and care

Known for its distinctive blue to green shades, often with dark ribbing or gold flecks. Real turquoise is very rare and may be substituted in crystal work with blue howlite. Do not immerse it, expose to sunlight or heat which will cause it to fade.

unakite

vulcanite

Unakite is a protective crystal and is useful in all matters relating to the protective realm. Use it in a grid, include in a beacon or place in the corners of the home. Good when worn as jewelry.

Vulcanite assists with any element in the awareness realm. It should be paired with a grounding stone. Vulcanite helps to repel negativity and attract positivity.

colors and care

Unakite is a combination of epidote (green) and feldspar (pink). It is very hard and is resistant to breaking and scratching. It can be immersed and exposed to sunlight.

colors and care

Look for vulcanite stones that combine dark gray, pink and pale blue mottled colors. It is often referred to as que sera. Vulcanite is quite soft and will break or scratch easily. It should not be exposed to heat or be immersed.

white selenite

White selenite crystals assist with any process that involves finding clear pathways and is very useful in the higher realm elements. It is best used in rough form in a grid or incorporated into a beacon.

colors and care

Often confused with clear quartz, white selenite is clear and colorless, resembling an ice cube. Some selenite is dyed to mimic other crystals. It is easily shattered, and should not be heated or immersed.

yellow opal

Yellow opal is the stone of endings and transformation, signaling that a new turn or opportunity is sought or on the horizon. It can be likened to the Tower card in the Tarot where its appearance means sudden and unsettling change is foretold.

In crystal work, yellow opal can be used to remove blockages and increase the flow of positive energy leading to new paths ahead.

colors and care

A variety of opal that is mostly opaque white with some inclusions of yellow or gold however it can also be found as bright yellow with heavy translucency. Easily scratched or shattered, do not heat or immerse.

how to set a grid

Building a crystal grid is a simple process and requires nothing more than a peaceful place and some thoughtful planning. While there are some commonalities, your grids can be simple or complex. They can be personal, for you only, however constructing grids with a group of friends can also be both fun and helpful.

Choose a time when you a free from interruptions or disturbances. Grids can be constructed indoors or outdoors (depending on the weather) but should have some sort of ambient light source nearby such as sunlight, ceiling light or a lampshade.

layouts

A basic grid layout has four corners and a central soul stone with focus stones placed in areas around it, according to what type of grid you are setting. In the later pages, you'll find some examples of grid layouts.

As you become familiar with the elements and master grid settings, you'll find the layouts that suit you best, depending on whether you are working on specific questions or just improvements in general. Timeframe grids, such as the lunar and astrological grids will help to set focus on events in the future, or attributes that surround the current day.

focus and purpose

Determine the purpose of the grid. Are you asking a central question? Or are you working on a specific problem or area of your spirituality? Anything is acceptable, as long as your grid has a focus and purpose.

alignment and grounding

First, layout a mat on which to construct your grid - a cotton or silk scarf would suffice depending on the size of your grid. If you practice grid work often, you may want to design a mat just for this purpose with the grid lines and points marked on it. Alternatively, you can use a bed of sand.

Next, using simple compass points, position your grid so that the points are aligned with the four major directions, north, south, east, and west.

Then ground your grid by containing it within the classical natural elements, represented as earth, air, fire, and water. In each of the corners place an object that represents the classical element. Position earth in the south point, air in the north point, fire in the east point and water in the west point.

earth	Use anything organic such as a freshly cut flower, a bunch of sweet herbs or a small pot of soil. You can also use the astrological symbols for Capricorn, Taurus or Virgo, or any pentacle card from the Tarot.
air	A feather is usually the best representation. You can also use the astrological symbols for Libra, Aquarius or Gemini, or any sword card from the Tarot.
fire	Use a small lit candle or tea light candle to signify fire. Be careful if leaving it unattended. You can also use the astrological symbols for Aries, Leo or Sagittarius, or any rod card from the Tarot.
water	Use a small bowl or container of unfiltered water. You can also use the astrological symbols for Cancer, Scorpio or Pisces, or any cup card from the Tarot.

setting the stones

Take some time choosing your crystals and consider where they will be placed in the grid.

soul stone	Choose a crystal that best represents you or your central question. Place it in the center point of the grid.
focus stones	Choose the elemental crystals from each of the crystal realms that relate to the grid's focus. Position them on the grid according to the type of grid you are constructing. You do not need to include every realm. Your focus stones can be supported by other stones.

centering and connecting

Once you have constructed your grid, take some time to sit in quiet meditation, clearing your mind of any thoughts that are not related to the grid's focus.

If you have trouble concentrating, use some simple meditation practices such as focusing on your breath, or play some quiet spiritual music. This is also a good time for prayer, affirmations or dedications.

Allow the energy of the crystals to wash over you so that you make a connection to the grid. Once you feel you have connected, you are free to go about your normal daily routine. Or you can choose to remain with the grid and simply meditate.

ending the grid

The energy of the grid will last until the next sunrise at which time you can deconstruct the grid. You can of course also deconstruct it before then, if you feel the energy has been depleted or it has served its purpose.

universals grid

The universals grid layout has five concentric circles which are then divided into each of the realms. Crystals can be placed accordingly. The energy realm surrounds all of the inner circles and crystals from this realm can be placed near the other realms for focus.

This is perhaps the most diverse grid as it allows you to focus on particular element combinations.

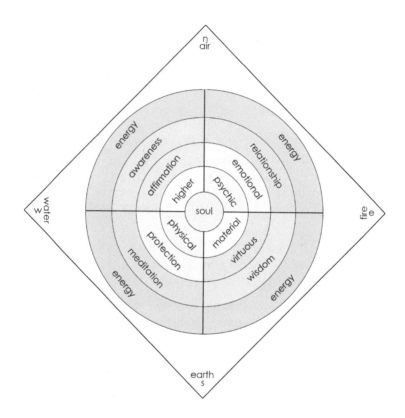

ley grid

The ley grid has eight ley lines radiating from the soul – north, south, east, west, south east, north west, south west and north east. Place crystals along the ley lines using any many lines as required. For example, to energize a relationship, place relationship crystals on the east line. To clear relationships of negative influences, place relationship crystals along the north line. To energize and ground a relationship, place relationship crystals on the southeast line.

You can use many of the same crystals along the ley lines, and use multiple lines with complementary elements, as needed.

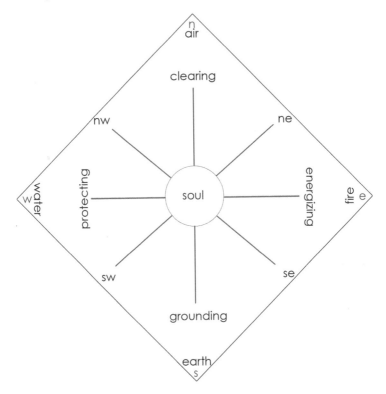

lunar grid

The lunar grid tracks phases of the moon. Set your grid according to the current moon phase. You can also use this grid to pass energy to elements in the coming month by setting crystals for upcoming events as they occur in the moon phase. For example, if you are buying a home today and the moon is currently in the first quarter, place crystals according to where important matters relating to the home occur, such as contract exchanges and moving in.

You can also set crystals in the solar day using the quadrants for the sun's position.

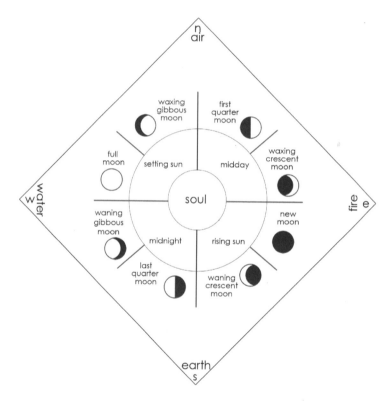

astrological grid

The astrological symbols in this grid are arranged according to their classical elements, each radiating from the soul stone. Use this grid to focus on months of the year where important events occur, or to focus on attributes related to the sun signs.

The 13th zodiac, ophiuchus, is the place of the "unknown" and can represent any period which is not yet determined. For example, a wedding for which a date has yet to be set, or an issue where the possibilities are unknown.

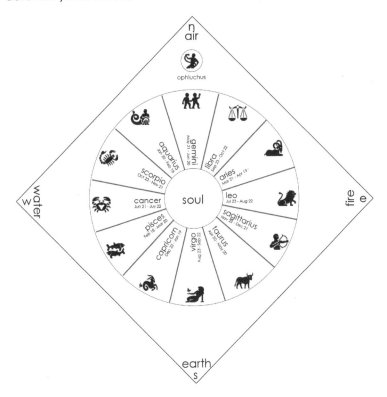

aura color chart

violet	connection understanding knowledge
indigo	psychic abilities imagination
blue	self-expression communication
green	love empathy compassion
yellow	power control clarity
orange	emotions creativity
red	instincts security

Aura colors can also be used in reference to chakras.

astrological crystals

aquarius Jan 21 – Feb 19	garnet
pisces Feb 20 – Mar 20	amethyst
aries Mar 21 – Apr 20	unakite
taurus Apr 21 – May 21	aura cobalt
gemini May 22 – Jun 21	agate
cancer Jun 22 – Jul 23	peridot
leo Jul 24 – Aug 23	black onyx
virgo Aug 24 – Sep 23	carnelian
libra Sep 24 – Oct 23	apatite
scorpio Oct 24 – Nov 22	aquamarine
sagittarius Nov 23 – Dec 21	clear quartz
capricorn Dec 22 – Jan 20	red jasper

crystal categories

clearing			
	agate	malachite	sardonyx
	apatite	optical calcite	serpentine
	black obsidian	orange calcite	sodalite
	cordierite	pink calcite	vulcanite
	jadeite	rhodonite	white selenite

energizing			
	amazonite	clear quartz	nuummite
	amethyst	clinochlore	orange selenite
	aquamarine	epidote	peridot
	black onyx	girasol	pietersite
	blue fluorite	goldstone	purple fluorite
	blue quartz	green fluorite	pyrite
	bronzite	hypersthene	red jasper
	carnelian	kunzite	rose quartz
	chalcedony	kyanite	smoky quartz
	cinnabarite	magnesite	snowflake obsidian
	citrine	mookaite	sunstone

grounding			
	ametrine	labradorite	scolecite
	aventurine	lapis lazuli	tiger's eye
	garnet	lepidolite	yellow opal
	hematite	moss agate	

protecting			
	chrysoprase	fuchsite	shungite
	cobalt aura	howlite	turquoise
	dumortierite	rhodochrosite	unakite

crystals a-z

agate	aura cleansing	©✖🔺◈♉
	aura strengthening	🥛🌟🍀✳
amazonite	calm	℮✖🔺◈♉
	energy amplification	
amethyst	intellect	℮✖🔺◈♉
	psychic energy	🥛✳
	vibration	
ametrine	brotherhood	𝒢✖🔺◈♉
	friendship	🥛✳
apatite	inner peace	©✖🔺◈
	truth	🌟🍀
aquamarine	clairalience	℮✖🔺◈♉
	clairaudience	🥛🌟🍀✳
	claircognizance	
	clairsentience	
	clairvoyance	
	mediumship	
	precognition	
	telepathy	
aventurine	fortune	𝒢✖🔺◈♉
	philanthropy	🥛🌟🍀✳
	prosperity	
black obsidian	clarity	©✖🔺◈
	fear	🥛🌟🍀✳
black onyx	spirit guardians	℮✖🔺◈♉
	spirit guides	🥛🌟🍀✳
	spiritual development	

blue fluorite	biorhythmic balance	
	energy equilibrium	
	life balance	
blue quartz	comfort	
	self esteem	
bronzite	addiction	
	self esteem	
carnelian	anger	
	manifested entities	
chalcedony	angelic	
	earthbound spirits	
	oversoul	
chrysoprase	fortune	
	prosperity	
cinnabarite	fortune	
	prosperity	
citrine	good luck	
clear quartz	affirmation	
	energy stimulation	
	manifestation	
clinochlore	angelic	
	spirit guides	
cobalt aura	blood flow	
	bones	
	immunity	
	inflammation	
cordierite	decisions	
	judgment	

dumortierite	astral travel	🇵 ✖ ⛰ ◈ ళ
	time travel	🥛 ✳ 🦪 ✳
epidote	abundance	ℯ ✖ ⛰ ◈ ళ
	allowance	🥛 ✳ 🦪
	potential	
fuchsite	ceremonial stability	🇵 ✖ ⛰ ◈ ళ
	manifested entities	🥛 ✳ 🦪 ✳
	psychic attack	
	psychic vampirism	
garnet	bones	🇬 ✖ ⛰ ◈ ళ
	general health	🥛 ✳ 🦪 ✳
	inflammation	
girasol	immunity	ℯ ✖ ⛰ ◈ ళ
	rebirth	🥛 ✳ 🦪
	regeneration	
goldstone	ascended masters	ℯ ✖ ⛰ ◈ ళ
	channeling	🥛 ✳ 🦪
	communication	
	mediumship	
	oversoul	
green fluorite	biorhythmic balance	ℯ ✖ ⛰ ◈
	energy equilibrium	
	inner peace	
	life balance	
hematite	ceremonial stability	🇬 ✖ ⛰ ◈ ళ
	egotism	🥛 ✳
	grounding	
	shamanic ritual	
howlite	daydreams	🇵 ✖ ⛰ ◈ ళ
	meditation	✳ 🦪
	peace	

hypersthene	ascension	⒠ ⊠ ▲ ◈ ♉
	empowerment	▽ ✺ ⚥ ✳
	will	

jadeite	break ties	⒞ ⊠ ▲ ◈ ♉
	cord cutting	✺
	emotional blockages	
	prejudice	
	worry	

kunzite	consciousness	⒠ ⊠ ▲ ◈ ♉
	happiness	
	illumination	
	lightbody	

kyanite	blood flow	⒠ ⊠ ▲ ◈ ♉
	comfort	✺
	grief	
	self-healing	

labradorite	akashic record	⒢ ⊠ ▲ ◈ ♉
	comprehension	▽ ✺ ⚥ ✳
	insight	

lapis lazuli	belonging	⒢ ⊠ ▲ ◈ ♉
	inner child	▽ ✺ ⚥ ✳
	past lives	
	reflection	

| lepidolite | allowance | ⒢ ⊠ ▲ ◈ ♉ |
| | perfection | |

magnesite	abundance	⒠ ⊠ ▲ ◈ ♉
	goodwill	✺ ⚥ ✳
	respect	
	unity	

| malachite | decisions | ⒞ ⊠ ▲ ◈ |
| | resolution | ✺ |

mookaite	brotherhood	
moss agate	awakening earthbound spirits spirit guardians	
nuummite	astral travel daydreams dreams intuition meditation time travel	
optical calcite	comprehension concentration dreams etheric body metaphysics	
orange calcite	clarity discipline forgiveness gratitude	
orange selenite	biorhythmic balance energy equilibrium life balance unity	
peridot	happiness illumination soul awakening	
pietersite	ascended masters brotherhood mother earth past lives rebirth	

pink calcite	acceptance	
	bonds	
	devotion	
	friendship	
	humanity	
	nurture	
	unity	

purple fluorite	energy amplification	
	kundalini energy	
	lightbody	
	metabolism	

pyrite	awakening	
	creativity	
	decisions	
	etheric body	
	potential	
	reincarnate	
	resolution	
	self esteem	
	truth	

red jasper	bonds	
	goddesses	
	mother earth	
	nurture	

rhodochrosite	aura strengthening	
	ceremonial stability	
	manifested entities	
	psychic attack	
	psychic vampirism	
	safety	
	shamanic ritual	

rhodonite	anger	⒞⊠▲◈♑
	animosity	🥛✿✳
	fear	
	negativity	
	peace	
	prejudice	

rose quartz	bonds	⒠⊠▲◈♑
	divine love	✳
	empathy	
	goodwill	
	self esteem	
	unconditional love	

sardonyx	awareness	⒞⊠▲◈♑
	christ consciousness	🥛✹✿✳
	consciousness	
	higher self	
	insight	
	karma	
	knowledge	
	mediumship	
	reflection	
	spiritual awareness	

scolecite	grounding	⒢⊠▲◈
	mental clarity	✹✿
	visualisation	

serpentine	negativity	⒞⊠▲◈
	respect	✹✳
	worry	

shungite	calm	ℙ⊠▲◈♑
	peace	🥛✹✿✳
	serenity	

smoky quartz	empowerment	ℯ ☒ ▲ ◈ ℘
	energy amplification	✳
	energy stimulation	
	kundalini energy	

snowflake obsidian	addiction	ℯ ☒ ▲ ◈
	discipline	▽ ☀ ♨ ✳
	judgment	
	resolution	

sodalite	apathy	ℭ ☒ ▲ ◈ ℘
	aura cleansing	
	emotional blockages	
	emotional stability	
	humility	

sunstone	aura strengthening	ℯ ☒ ▲ ◈ ℘
	lightbody	▽ ☀ ♨ ✳
	selflessness	

tiger's eye	grounding	ℐ ☒ ▲ ◈ ℘
	mother earth	▽ ☀ ♨ ✳
	perfection	
	spirit guardians	

turquoise	blood flow	ℙ ☒ ▲ ◈ ℘
	bones	✳
	general health	
	immunity	
	inflammation	
	metabolism	

unakite	ceremonial stability	ℙ ☒ ▲ ◈ ℘
	manifested entities	▽ ☀ ♨ ✳
	psychic attack	
	psychic vampirism	
	shamanic ritual	

vulcanite	awareness	CX▲◈℘
	celestial	☀
	karma	
	requests	
	spiritual awareness	

| white selenite | blessings | CX▲◈℘ |
| | devas | ☀ |

yellow opal	rebirth	ℰX▲◈℘
	reincarnate	☀
	soul awakening	

elements a-z

abundance	affirmation	epidote
		magnesite
acceptance	virtuous	pink calcite
addiction	virtuous	bronzite
		snowflake obsidian
affirmation	affirmation	clear quartz
akashic record	wisdom	labradorite
allowance	virtuous	epidote
		lepidolite
angelic	higher	chalcedony
		clinochlore
anger	virtuous	carnelian
		rhodonite
animosity	virtuous	rhodonite
apathy	virtuous	sodalite
ascended masters	higher	goldstone
		pietersite
ascension	higher	hypersthene
astral travel	higher	dumortierite
		nuummite
aura cleansing	higher	agate
		sodalite
aura strengthening	protection	agate
		rhodochrosite
		sunstone
awakening	higher	moss agate
		pyrite

awareness	awareness	sardonyx
		vulcanite
belonging	emotional	lapis lazuli
biorhythmic balance	energy	blue fluorite
		green fluorite
		orange selenite
blessings	higher	white selenite
blood flow	physical	cobalt aura
		kyanite
		turquoise
bonds	relationship	pink calcite
		red jasper
		rose quartz
bones	physical	cobalt aura
		garnet
		turquoise
break ties	relationship	jadeite
brotherhood	relationship	ametrine
		mookaite
		pietersite
calm	emotional	amazonite
		shungite
celestial	higher	vulcanite
ceremonial stability	protection	fuchsite
		hematite
		rhodochrosite
		unakite
channeling	meditation	goldstone
christ consciousness	higher	sardonyx

clairalience	psychic	aquamarine
clairaudience	psychic	aquamarine
claircognizance	psychic	aquamarine
clairsentience	psychic	aquamarine
clairvoyance	psychic	aquamarine
clarity	wisdom	black obsidian orange calcite
comfort	emotional	blue quartz kyanite
communication	wisdom	goldstone
comprehension	wisdom	labradorite optical calcite
concentration	wisdom	optical calcite
consciousness	awareness	kunzite sardonyx
cord cutting	higher	jadeite
creativity	affirmation	pyrite
daydreams	meditation	howlite nuummite
decisions	wisdom	cordierite malachite pyrite
devas	higher	white selenite
devotion	virtuous	pink calcite
discipline	virtuous	orange calcite snowflake obsidian
divine love	emotional	rose quartz

dreams	higher	nuummite
		optical calcite
earthbound spirits	higher	chalcedony
		moss agate
egotism	virtuous	hematite
emotional blockages	emotional	jadeite
		sodalite
emotional stability	emotional	sodalite
empathy	virtuous	rose quartz
empowerment	affirmation	hypersthene
		smoky quartz
energy amplification	energy	amazonite
		purple fluorite
		smoky quartz
energy equilibrium	energy	blue fluorite
		green fluorite
		orange selenite
energy stimulation	energy	clear quartz
		smoky quartz
etheric body	higher	optical calcite
		pyrite
fear	virtuous	black obsidian
		rhodonite
forgiveness	virtuous	orange calcite
fortune	material	aventurine
		chrysoprase
		cinnabarite
friendship	relationship	ametrine
		pink calcite

general health	physical	garnet
		turquoise
goddesses	higher	red jasper
good luck	material	citrine
goodwill	virtuous	magnesite
		rose quartz
gratitude	virtuous	orange calcite
grief	emotional	kyanite
grounding	protection	hematite
		scolecite
		tiger's eye
happiness	emotional	kunzite
		peridot
higher self	awareness	sardonyx
humanity	virtuous	pink calcite
humility	virtuous	sodalite
illumination	awareness	kunzite
		peridot
immunity	physical	cobalt aura
		girasol
		turquoise
inflammation	physical	cobalt aura
		garnet
		turquoise
inner child	higher	lapis lazuli
inner peace	affirmation	apatite
		green fluorite
insight	wisdom	labradorite
		sardonyx

intellect	wisdom	amethyst
intuition	awareness	nuummite
judgment	virtuous	cordierite
		snowflake obsidian
karma	higher	sardonyx
		vulcanite
knowledge	higher	sardonyx
kundalini energy	energy	purple fluorite
		smoky quartz
life balance	energy	blue fluorite
		green fluorite
		orange selenite
lightbody	energy	kunzite
		purple fluorite
		sunstone
manifestation	material	clear quartz
manifested entities	protection	carnelian
		fuchsite
		rhodochrosite
		unakite
meditation	meditation	howlite
		nuummite
mediumship	psychic	aquamarine
		goldstone
		sardonyx
mental clarity	wisdom	scolecite
metabolism	physical	purple fluorite
		turquoise
metaphysics	higher	optical calcite

mother earth	higher	pietersite
		red jasper
		tiger's eye
negativity	protection	rhodonite
		serpentine
nurture	virtuous	pink calcite
		red jasper
oversoul	higher	chalcedony
		goldstone
past lives	awareness	lapis lazuli
		pietersite
peace	virtuous	howlite
		rhodonite
		shungite
perfection	virtuous	lepidolite
		tiger's eye
philanthropy	material	aventurine
potential	awareness	epidote
		pyrite
precognition	psychic	aquamarine
prejudice	virtuous	jadeite
		rhodonite
prosperity	material	aventurine
		chrysoprase
		cinnabarite
psychic attack	protection	fuchsite
		rhodochrosite
		unakite
psychic energy	psychic	amethyst

psychic vampirism	protection	fuchsite
		rhodochrosite
		unakite
rebirth	energy	girasol
		pietersite
		yellow opal
reflection	awareness	lapis lazuli
		sardonyx
regeneration	wisdom	girasol
reincarnate	higher	pyrite
		yellow opal
requests	affirmation	vulcanite
resolution	wisdom	malachite
		pyrite
		snowflake obsidian
respect	virtuous	magnesite
		serpentine
safety	virtuous	rhodochrosite
self esteem	emotional	blue quartz
		bronzite
		pyrite
		rose quartz
self-healing	emotional	kyanite
selflessness	awareness	sunstone
serenity	affirmation	shungite
shamanic ritual	protection	hematite
		rhodochrosite
		unakite

soul awakening	awareness	peridot
		yellow opal
spirit guardians	higher	black onyx
		moss agate
		tiger's eye
spirit guides	higher	black onyx
		clinochlore
spiritual awareness	awareness	sardonyx
		vulcanite
spiritual development	awareness	black onyx
telepathy	psychic	aquamarine
time travel	higher	dumortierite
		nuummite
truth	virtuous	apatite
		pyrite
unconditional love	relationship	rose quartz
unity	relationship	magnesite
		orange selenite
		pink calcite
vibration	higher	amethyst
visualisation	meditation	scolecite
will	virtuous	hypersthene
worry	emotional	jadeite
		serpentine